MADAME ENDORA'S BOOK OF FORTUNES

MONOLITH GRAPHICS
CLEVELAND, OHIO, USA
WWW.MONOLITHGRAPHICS.COM

PUBLISHED BY MONOLITH GRAPHICS
CLEVELAND, OHIO, USA
WWW.MONOLITHGRAPHICS.COM

Publisher's Cataloging-in-Publication Data
Madame Endora's Book of Fortunes
by Joseph Vargo and Christine Filipak

ISBN 9780982489956
1. non-fiction, divination, tarot
2. Vargo, Joseph
3. Filipak, Christine

May your path be blissful and prosperous.

MADAME ENDORA'S FORTUNE CARDS

MADAME ENDORA'S WISDOM OF THE AGES

A MYSTICAL HISTORY

Since the dawn of civilization, mankind has looked beyond the mortal realm to seek guidance along life's path. Throughout history, people of every culture have utilized a variety of techniques to attune themselves to the spirit world and the unseen powers that surround us. Signs and omens appear in many forms and have been interpreted in a wide variety of ways through the ages. The Druids of ancient England were said to gaze into flames of sacrificial fires to see the future. Greek oracles used pools of water for scrying to forecast the outcomes of battles and important events. Medieval alchemists and seers were said to use crystals to channel energy and commune with spirits, and gypsy fortune tellers utilized tea leaves, palmistry and astrology to reveal a person's destiny and guide them along the path to prosperity, inner peace and true love.

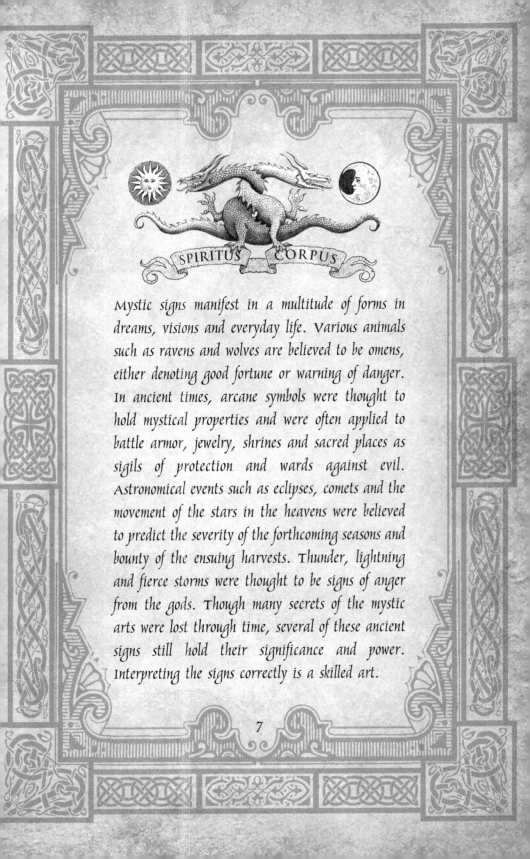

SPIRITUS · CORPUS

Mystic signs manifest in a multitude of forms in dreams, visions and everyday life. Various animals such as ravens and wolves are believed to be omens, either denoting good fortune or warning of danger. In ancient times, arcane symbols were thought to hold mystical properties and were often applied to battle armor, jewelry, shrines and sacred places as sigils of protection and wards against evil. Astronomical events such as eclipses, comets and the movement of the stars in the heavens were believed to predict the severity of the forthcoming seasons and bounty of the ensuing harvests. Thunder, lightning and fierce storms were thought to be signs of anger from the gods. Though many secrets of the mystic arts were lost through time, several of these ancient signs still hold their significance and power. Interpreting the signs correctly is a skilled art.

7

MADAME ENDORA'S FORTUNE CARDS

The true origins of fortune telling cards are shrouded in mystery. They are believed to hearken back to ancient Egypt where they were said to be based on the Book Of Thoth, a tome of spiritual knowledge written by the god of wisdom. Various decks of fortune cards have existed through the centuries, utilizing a wide array of themes and images to symbolize people and events in our everyday life. Divination by cards has endured the ages to become the most popular and widespread means of fortune telling in the modern day.

Combining mythological lore, Old World secrets and mystic symbolism, Madame Endora's Fortune Cards offer insightful advice concerning matters of love, money, health and general prosperity. This unique oracle deck utilizes symbolism from several ancient dynasties and esoteric cultures, including Egyptian, Celtic, and Medieval imagery, as well as heraldic designs from the legendary realm of fable. The cards depict some of the most powerful amulets, talismans, charms and spirit totems from history using iconic images to convey universal concepts that can easily be recognized and understood. Many of the messages present advice for current or future situations while others simply offer positive reinforcement of lessons learned from past experience.

Each card offers a simple fortune that requires no interpretation, allowing the reader to receive an instant message concerning their immediate future. In addition, the cards may be used in a variety of spreads to achieve more in-depth readings utilizing the deck's full divinatory potential. While some of the cards depict influential people and factors in a person's life, others reveal how to unlock answers regarding current issues through inner reflection and by adapting a different outlook toward a given situation. Because interpretations vary depending on the personal factors surrounding an individual, the cards speak to each reader in their own way. It is always important to keep an open mind when deciphering the meaning of the cards. Intuition is a powerful force that should be heeded at all times to attain the best outcome in any circumstance.

May your path be blissful and prosperous.

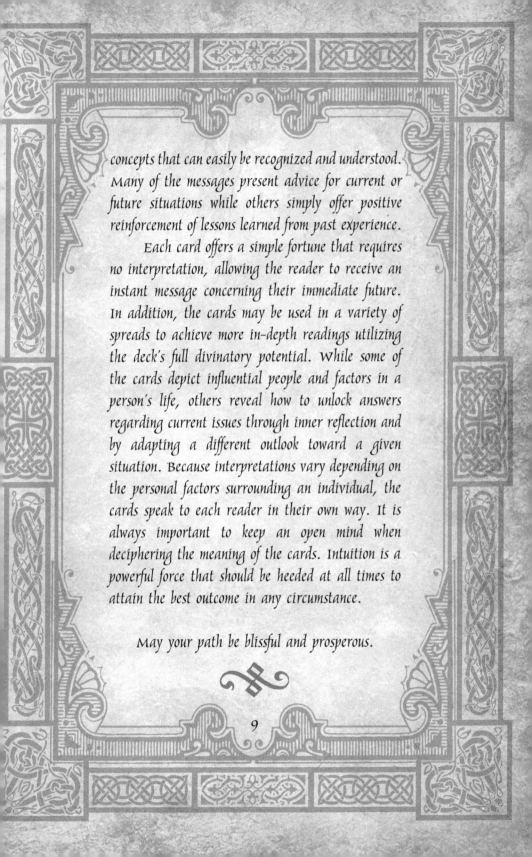

THE ROYAL COURT

The Royal Court consists of 8 cards that represent the most powerful personal influences in your life. Certain cards may symbolize an actual person, while others may reveal mindsets that should be adopted or actions that should be taken to affect your own destiny. The Royal Court holds sway over the mortal realm by offering tangible advice and guidance and recommending actions that are within your power. Each member of The Royal Court possesses unique wisdom concerning their specific position or caste, based on knowledge, skills and experience. The expertise of The Royal Court is invaluable and should be closely heeded and taken to heart.

THE KING

AUTHORITY
AND DIPLOMACY

The King

An Egyptian pharaoh sits upon his golden throne before an inscribed backdrop of ancient gods, designating him as the earthly avatar of supreme universal powers. His right hand is raised in a gesture of peace and respect, signifying his considerate nature, while his left hand holds a jeweled scepter, a symbol of his royal status, and an ankh, the symbol of life and strength.

The King represents a dominant and revered male influence. As patriarch of The Royal Court, The King symbolizes a father figure as well as someone in a position of authority. A distinguished and wise man, The King is a natural leader who can assess and take charge of any situation. He is, at times, a lawmaker and judge, and must balance power with thoughtful diplomacy. The King also represents great wealth and inheritance, reminding us of the newfound responsibilities that come with such riches.

The King is the reigning alpha male and will rise above others to lead them with his unwavering confidence and superior skills, controlling all matters and resolving any problems by wisely utilizing the forces at his command. The King may have inherited his position or risen to his lofty status by triumphing over former controlling powers. He uses his wealth of experience to preside over matters requiring diplomacy, balancing wisdom with action. The King's decisions are just and final, but they are reached through thoughtful consideration of all surrounding circumstances. The King values honesty and loyalty above all and may be swayed with sincere acts and thoughtful words.

THE QUEEN

LOVE AND PROSPERITY

The Queen

The Queen represents a dominant female influence that is compassionate, intelligent and strong-willed. She is a respected and refined woman who is sympathetic and nurturing, yet emotionally confident.

As matriarch of The Royal Court, The Queen also embodies love and fertility. In matters of the heart, The Queen represents a very positive omen. She symbolizes love that may either be a simple deep bond, or a friendship that blossoms into romantic feelings over time. In matters of fertility, The Queen denotes healthy childbirth as well as an increase in creativity and personal productivity. She reminds us that by nurturing our ideas and allowing them to flourish, they will soon take on a life of their own.

Whereas The King commands physical matters, The Queen governs the emotional aspects that influence one's life. She presides over affairs of passion and settles disputes through calm reason and thoughtful compromise. The Queen remains dignified in the most dire circumstances. She may seem overly protective at times, but she has only the best intentions for her children and loyal subjects, therefore her maternal instincts should be closely heeded.

The Queen is the herald of prosperity, signifying a time of physical and emotional well-being as well as increased wealth. Above all, The Queen reminds us to take time to appreciate those we love and live life to the fullest.

THE WIZARD

USE YOUR SKILLS TO AID OTHERS

The Wizard

An ancient wizard gazes longingly into the dark unknown. His right hand is encircled by a glowing halo as he channels the magical energy of the universe. His left hand holds a wooden staff ornamented with a crystal orb, symbolizing the powers of the earth. Golden knotwork adorns his attire, suggestive of the intricate weavings of magic. Mystic symbols surround him with an aura of arcane power, allowing him to command the forces of nature. His elderly eyes appear clouded, yet he has great clarity of vision in the mystic realm.

As sage and mystic of The Royal Court, The Wizard represents a wise person who offers assistance in matters that are beyond another's expertise. Mysterious and charismatic, he possesses a charming demeanor. A philosopher and advisor, The Wizard is also a skilled practitioner of the known sciences and the art of magic.

In Arthurian lore, the wizard Merlin was a mysterious hermit who used magic to help the rightful king rise to power and claim the throne of England. The Wizard also guided the king and used his powers to help him in his darkest hours. By confiding in Merlin and trusting his wisdom, the king overcame all obstacles and ascended to legendary heights.

The Wizard has the ability to manifest our innermost wishes and resolve matters that seem impossible or hopeless. The Wizard's power is derived from secret knowledge and the wisdom to use it discerningly, however an abuse of such power can lead to misfortune. Use your skills to aid others and together you will achieve great things.

THE SEER

FOLLOW YOUR INTUITION

The Seer

A beautiful woman stands before a wheel of astrological symbols representing her unearthly knowledge and vision concerning the affairs of men. In the hierarchy of The Royal Court, The Seer uses her arcane insight to advise The King and The Queen in all matters and they in turn use their wisdom to determine the correct course of action for the greatest benefit of their subjects.

The Seer is a spiritual advisor, well-versed in occult knowledge and the mystical arts. She is a gifted prophet who can see the future clearly. The Seer's scope is limitless. Nothing can deceive her or obstruct her vision. When The Seer is present, all hidden truths will be revealed. The Seer also reminds us to trust our instincts and natural intuition.

The Seer guides us by helping us to avoid certain obstacles, allowing us to recognize and follow the path of our true destiny. Though depicted as a female, The Seer may also represent a male influence who looks after your best interest or offers insightful advice. Such wisdom should be heeded, even if it advises against your desired course of action. The Seer's guidance may reveal markers along life's path or warn of impending perils, depending on its proximity to other cards in a reading.

The Seer may also represent a spiritual sign such as a prophetic dream that directs you toward a goal or warns of dangers to avoid. Those who heed The Seer's advice may not attain their immediate desires, however the end goal will be more rewarding. The Seer can look beyond the present to view the outcome of current dilemmas and relationships, as well as health and financial issues. The Seer's advice may at times be difficult to understand or follow, but the path of destiny is seldom clear and is often clouded by a variety of distractions.

THE KNIGHT

TRIUMPH OVER ADVERSITY

The Knight

A medieval knight in shining armor sits atop his rearing steed, sword raised and ready for battle. His gleaming blade acts as a formidable weapon against injustice, while his armor protects him from harm. His golden shield bears the likeness of the phoenix, a symbol of an indomitable adversary.

A gallant protector and warrior, The Knight possesses a courageous and competitive spirit. He is the champion of justice and the symbol of triumph over adversity. The Knight is a loyal guardian and serves his king and queen, acting on their behalf at all times. Knights of legend were defenders of the realm that were said to battle dragons, giants and other monstrous beasts. Though customarily male, The Knight may also symbolize a strong female who rises to the aid of a worthy cause.

The Knight is the avatar of chivalry, displaying great courtesy and high moral standards. He is a valiant crusader and a seeker of truth, sworn to right the injustices of the world. The Knight is selfless and lives by a code of honor, valiantly putting the needs of others before his own and defending those who cannot defend themselves.

The Knight's great physical strength is matched by his fierce determination, courage and loyalty. The Knight may represent someone who comes to your rescue to take your side when you face insurmountable odds. The Knight reminds us to take up noble causes and selflessly fight for what is right. Be direct when dealing with others and meet matters head-on. Make sure you are fully prepared before engaging in battle.

THE MAIDEN

A NEW RELATIONSHIP BLOSSOMS

The Maiden

A beautiful young woman resides in the comfort of her ivory tower. She gazes longingly at the unexplored world outside and dreams of the wonders it holds. Her delicate hand holds a single rose, a symbol of blossoming beauty. Though she is alone and confined to her tower, she is safe and sheltered from the corrupting forces of the world around her.

Young and naive, The Maiden embodies innocence, purity and hope. She represents loyal friendship and emotional longing. The Maiden is the herald of good intentions and offers honest advice in a sincere and helpful way. She focuses solely on the positive and sees the best potential in all things. Due to her lack of worldly experience, her outlook might be somewhat unrealistic at times, but her thoughts come directly from the heart.

The Maiden may also represent the camaraderie of sisterhood or a close bond with a trusted female friend. Unlike the strong-willed Queen, The Maiden possesses a fragile ego and may be hurt by harsh words or acts of rejection. Due to her innocent nature, she can be easily seduced, deceived or led astray by hollow words.

The Maiden also signifies the beginning of a new relationship or a fresh start to an unfulfilled pursuit. She may be prone to flights of fancy, but her dreams act as inspiration to achieve higher goals. The Maiden's optimistic outlook reminds us to take time to appreciate the beauty in the world.

THE MINSTREL

LET YOUR INTENTIONS
BE KNOWN

The Minstrel

A medieval bard serenades his audience, sharing emotional tales and enriching the lives of all who cross his path. The Minstrel is a poet and musician who sings heartfelt ballads and songs of good cheer. He represents a harmonious union as well as musical and artistic creativity.

The Minstrel enlightens those whose hearts he touches. He is a master storyteller, adept in all forms of entertainment. The Minstrel professes his thoughts and intentions for all to hear, but has a tendency to have a jaded outlook and often wears his heart on his sleeve.

The Minstrel is the entertainer of The Royal Court, exuding a commanding presence whenever he takes the stage to perform. He is a gifted wordsmith and can make any news sound more enthralling and dramatic. The Minstrel expresses himself in a captivating way and can sway people by appealing to their emotions. In this regard The Minstrel can seduce others to fulfill his own desires.

The Minstrel lends guidance through insightful poetry and song lyrics while the soothing qualities of his music offer a relaxing diversion from the hectic world. He focuses on the romantic aspects of life while ignoring the mundane. The Minstrel boldly declares his innermost thoughts, advising us to let our intentions be known, loudly and clearly. Now is the time to voice your opinions and share your gifts with others.

THE HARLEQUIN

TRUE FEELINGS ARE MASKED

The Harlequin

A simple theater mask is accented by a border of ornate flourishes denoting the elaborate mysteries that lie beneath the concealing facade. The painted smile and tears combine the concepts of the traditional comedy and tragedy masks, denoting a wide range of emotions that may be employed to carry out a dramatic charade.

The Harlequin is an actor whose true feelings are masked in order to gain acceptance. At times, The Harlequin is a prankster whose sense of humor and playful acts make him the center of attention, however, The Harlequin may also be concealing a sadness derived from loneliness, loss or a broken heart.

The Harlequin appeases The Royal Court by pretending to be something he is not. The masked figure may represent either a male or female who diverts the truth through acts of deception. As in the Tarot, The Harlequin may also represent you as the player on life's stage. If you have strong emotions regarding a current situation, this may be a time to keep your feelings to yourself.

The Harlequin may represent a secret admirer who has developed hidden feelings for you or a jealous rival who pretends to be your friend. Accept nothing at face value, look deeper to discover what lies beneath the facade. Be careful who you confide in and keep your innermost desires hidden at this time.

THE REALM OF FABLE

The Realm of Fable consists of 10 cards that depict various beings from ancient lore. These strange and fantastic personifications from Egyptian, Celtic and Greek mythology represent outside forces that guide, motivate, hinder, or otherwise affect your destiny. Many of the denizens of The Realm Of Fable have legendary powers that manifest themselves as outside influences that can affect your fate, either directly or indirectly. By heeding the guidance of The Realm Of Fable, you will be better prepared to deal with any personal challenges that may arise along your path.

THE GOLEM

A CLOSE FRIEND ACTS ON YOUR BEHALF

The Golem

A bronze knight clutches a great sword in its armored hands. Its eyes shine with an eerie green light and its armor radiates an unearthly glow, symbolizing the mystical power that energizes it. The Golem solemnly stands guard before a sealed gate, signifying its protective nature and its steadfast dedication to its mission.

The Golem represents one who is indentured or motivated to do your bidding, such as a loyal friend who acts on your behalf or puts your interests before their own. When abused, The Golem may become an instrument of vengeance or destruction, however, such actions will often trigger harmful repercussions. In mythology, a golem was a creature formed from clay and brought to life through mystic words. Once alive, the golem was a slave to its master's commands.

As a faithful and trusted minion, The Golem will heedlessly serve your interests, granting your every desire while expecting nothing in return. The Golem signifies mindless devotion. It may represent someone to whom you have delegated specific responsibilities or someone who represents you in your absence.

The Golem may also symbolize someone who may be easily swayed. If this person admires or respects you, their opinions or personality may be shaped by your words. With the proper motivation, The Golem will serve you well in your time of need.

THE GREENMAN

THE FORCES OF NATURE FAVOR YOU

The Greenman

This graven face depicting the wise spirit of the forest is an ancient guardian that keeps watch over sacred places. The Greenman represents a deep reverence for all living things and guides us to follow this peaceful path. The Greenman protects all wildlife and imparts his blessings upon those who respect and cherish nature.

The Greenman is a symbol of the rebirth that occurs each spring after the harsh winter season. In this regard, The Greenman represents rejuvenation and a time of spiritual or physical growth after a period of rest or dormancy. The Greenman may also signify the fruition of a project or relationship, especially one that has developed gradually over a period of time.

The Greenman's howling expression is inspired by The Mouth of Truth, an ancient stone head with a gaping mouth that is said to bite the hands of liars. In this respect, The Greenman symbolizes the virtues of honesty and warns of the dire consequences for dishonesty.

The Greenman heralds natural creativity, exemplifying the need to draw from your roots and utilize the resources of your present surroundings in order to flourish. The Greenman also signifies a return to basics and an appreciation of the simple things in life, such as the natural beauty of the outdoors. The Greenman is a positive sign that your current endeavors will be productive if you simply allow nature to take its course.

HINDRANCE

FATE HAS BLOCKED THIS PATH FOR YOU

Hindrance

A woodland faerie rests upon a fallen tree, blocking the forest path. The crystal ball she holds allows her to see all possibilities concerning your journey, enabling her to determine that the path you are on is not the best route for you to follow. Some may see Hindrance as an insurmountable obstacle, while others see it as a challenge to accept.

Hindrance presents an unavoidable delay, however this is merely a temporary setback. If the current direction you are heading seems to be leading to a dead end, pause to consider your options, analyze your remaining possibilities and choose an alternate route to reach your desired destination. View the problem from a fresh perspective and try another approach to attaining your goal. Hindrance is not an end to your journey, only a diversion from your intended course. Hindrance forces us to leave the safety of the familiar, well-traveled road and venture into unexplored territory. Such avenues often present brighter prospects and newfound opportunities.

Hindrance may also represent a relationship that has reached a point of stagnation due to circumstances beyond your control. If you are not content in your current situation, yet unable to move forward, the time has come to pursue other options. Hindrance reminds us that the path to success is seldom the simplest road to travel. It is often filled with pitfalls to be avoided and obstacles to be overcome. Stop wasting time and energy on a lost cause, but don't lose sight of your goal. Pursue a different path and let nothing deter you from attaining your heart's desires.

MEDUSA

JEALOUSY LEADS TO DOWNFALL

Medusa

An exotic snake-haired woman with reptilian eyes allows a deadly serpent to constrict around her arm. In Greek mythology, Medusa was a young maiden whose beauty rivaled that of the Goddess Athena. In a jealous rage, Athena transformed the lovely mortal into a monstrous creature with serpents for hair. Anyone who gazed upon Medusa's frightening visage would instantly be turned to stone.

Medusa represents extreme envy and a corruption of beauty. Her tragic tale reminds us of the terrible consequences of jealousy. Often referred to as the "Green-eyed monster," jealousy takes its toll in repulsive ways. Those who act out of jealousy are destined to damage their own reputation, thus making themselves appear less attractive to others. Medusa may also signify an act of jealous rage, exile or harsh punishment. Be wary that someone may harbor resentful feelings toward you due to your enviable traits or possessions. In extreme instances, Medusa delivers a warning that someone who is jealous of you may be scheming to act against you.

Excessive jealousy leads to inevitable downfall. The natural instinct to desire better things drives us to work harder, but if that desire turns into obsessive jealousy, it can stifle forward progress on life's path. Jealousy is an unattractive character flaw that is repugnant to all who witness it. Do not allow petty envy to twist your heart. Jealous thoughts only distract attention away from important matters. Waste no time coveting things that belong to others. Instead, count your own blessings and appreciate the good things in your life.

THE SATYR

REVELRY AND INDULGENCE

The Satyr

The satyrs of Greek mythology were lustful woodland deities, half man, half goat, who filled their lives with wine, women and song, spending their time drinking, dancing, and cavorting with nymphs. The Satyr is playful, mischievous and prone to overindulgence. He is a symbol of music, dance, revelry and celebration. The Satyr also represents decadent, lewd behavior, unbridled fantasies, and lustful desires.

The Satyr exemplifies shedding your inhibitions and indulging your wildest whims to enjoy life to the fullest. Now is the time to partake in activities that are self-gratifying and unrestrained. Attend a party or concert and indulge your repressed desires or appetites. If you are stressed or burdened with work, unwinding with carefree pursuits will clear your mind and relieve tension.

Living only to satisfy your own desires may offer immediate gratification, but such actions may have damaging consequences in the long run. Indulging in excessive vices will eventually take a harsh toll on your mind and body and may prove harmful to your reputation.

The Satyr symbolizes a frivolous celebration or wild actions, free from the restraints of the mundane world. The Satyr may manifest as carefree merriment or as a passionate interaction based solely on wanton physical desires. The Satyr signifies a total disregard of consequences. He lives only for the moment and celebrates every day as if it were his last. Indulge in revelry and enjoy all of life's pleasures, but be aware of the repercussions for such activities.

SEDUCTION

PASSION AND
ROMANCE AWAIT

Seduction

A lovely enchantress strikes an alluring pose as she offers forth the mysterious contents of her jeweled goblet. The enticing aroma of her love potion wafts from the decanter beside her, drifting through the air to ensnare the unwary in her spell.

Seduction foretells that passion and romance await. Your sex appeal is at its height and unbridled sensuality weaves an irresistible spell. Secret fantasies manifest themselves through love letters and romantic gestures. Seduction awakens and rouses strong feelings that may have lain dormant or repressed for some time. Now is the time to stoke the fires of passion with a new relationship or rekindle an old flame that has dwindled or been long-extinguished.

Seduction is the act of appealing to someone's innermost desires as a means to attain their cooperation or support. It is a subtle art of persuasion that attains results through establishing a bond of confidence with the promise of great rewards. Skillful seduction will enable you to sway others to your way of thinking by connecting with them on a deeply personal level.

Where matters of the heart are concerned, Seduction signifies sensual actions or words that break down formal barriers and stimulate intimacy. This will often have pleasurable results and may lead to a romantic relationship, however, be wary of those who attempt to seduce you only to satisfy their own desires.

SERENDIPITY

BRIGHT NEW PROSPECTS
ARE ON THE HORIZON

Serendipity

A butterfly spirit from the realm of the fay shares a tender moment with a kindred spirit from the physical world. This night faerie represents a beneficial occurrence that arises through fortunate happenstance and perfect timing. Serendipity is an unexpected yet favorable turn of events. It may manifest as a chance meeting or discovery that results in something positive.

Serendipity signifies a happy accident or a lucky mistake that garners fortunate results. As one door closes another opens. In some instances, an act of serendipity may keep you safe from harm. Serendipity cannot be controlled or foreseen. It is a mysterious intervention of fate that leads to a surprisingly positive outcome, such as a fortuitous crossing of paths that has beneficial results for both parties.

Serendipity makes the best of any situation, resulting in an unexpectedly favorable outcome. Serendipity may manifest over a period of time as a series of events that fall into place for your benefit. What you may deem as misfortune will have positive ramifications in the long run. In this regard, the circumstances surrounding a loss may have repercussions that result in a gain.

Serendipity is a subtle reminder that all things happen for a reason. It is a sign that you are exactly where you were meant to be at this moment in your life. Being in the right place at the perfect time will allow you to capitalize on fleeting opportunities. Now is the time to take a chance and pursue a dream from the past. Bright new prospects are on the horizon.

THE SIREN

A TEMPTATION MAY
LEAD YOU ASTRAY

The Siren

A beautiful mermaid beckons with open arms, summoning unwary victims to her embrace. This bewitching sea nymph embodies a mysterious and spellbinding influence that promises great rewards. The Siren represents enchantment, dangerous allure and a captivating stimulus that incites foolish risk.

In ancient lore, The Siren's hypnotic call was irresistible, luring sailors away from their intended course to meet a dismal fate. In this regard, The Siren may warn that you are being led astray from your true destiny. This may manifest as a compelling force that diverts you from progressing in your intended direction. Be cautious when dealing with an irresistibly charming person and be wary not to follow them down a dangerous path. Keep a safe distance from the lure of forbidden desires.

The Siren represents seductive words or actions that stimulate inner passions with the promise of something that is extremely desirable, yet inevitably unattainable. Her hypnotic song exerts a charming spell over all who hear it. In this regard, The Siren represents voicing your desires in a charismatic and appealing way to create an irresistible offer. The Siren may also represent the intervention of mysterious forces that lead you blindly into unknown realms. This may manifest as misguided advice that keeps you from making the correct decision concerning important matters.

The Siren symbolizes the use of flattery and sex appeal to seduce others into acting against their own best interest. The Siren's allure is strong enough to convince those who fall beneath her spell to ignore common sense. Resist temptation.

THE SPHINX

CHOOSE YOUR WORDS CAREFULLY

The Sphinx

A wise and ancient creature from Greek and Egyptian mythology, The Sphinx devoured anyone who could not answer its perplexing riddle. This ominous tale acts as a warning to those who would venture into unknown territory without being fully prepared. The Sphinx foretells that your abilities will be tested. A difficult problem requires thoughtful contemplation. Don't act on impulse. Take time to consider all factors and options before making a decision.

The Sphinx poses a perplexing dilemma that can only be resolved through creative thinking. In this regard, a seemingly impossible task may be achieved by applying innovative ideas. The Sphinx warns to choose your words carefully and think before you speak. Be tactful when dealing with someone who has a reputation of being demanding or judgmental. Learn from the mistakes of others and rise to the challenges of a current situation.

The Sphinx stresses the importance of clear conversation. When speaking with authority figures, respond appropriately in a concise and informed manner. Gather your facts before saying something you may regret. Do not attempt to be deceptive or misleading in any way. Collect your thoughts and strategically prepare your ideas. Listen closely and fully understand what is asked of you before responding. Thoughtful words will allow you to progress in your desired direction.

THE SPIRIT

UNSEEN FORCES WATCH OVER YOU

The Spirit

A golden-winged angel holds a human skull and contemplates the mortal realm with loving interest. The Spirit is a watchful protector, possessing great wisdom and compassion, that lends guidance and comfort during trying times. Though The Spirit does not directly intervene in personal affairs, it is an ever-present influence that gently guides us toward making the right choices in life.

The Spirit represents a guardian angel or spirit of a loved one who watches over you. The Spirit may manifest itself in the form of a consoling friend who comes to your aid in a time of need. The Spirit acts as a protector to keep you safe from harm, guiding you along the correct path and steering you away from any looming dangers. Because the Spirit's scope of vision is vast, it may direct you away from something you currently desire for your own good. In this regard, apparent setbacks may have long-term benefits. All things happen for a reason.

The Spirit represents a higher power that has your best interests in mind. It will often make its presence known through personally significant signs that may go unnoticed by others. Though you may never fully interpret The Spirit's intent, you may feel its benevolent influence in subtle ways. The Spirit's vigilant guidance may manifest as a persistent inner voice that directs you toward achieving your goals and prevents you from making harmful choices. Do not ignore any intuitive feelings. Heed the signs and take heart in knowing that you are not alone.

THE BESTIARY

The Bestiary consists of 10 cards that represent various creatures of legend and superstition. Valuable lessons and truths can be discovered by reducing human character traits to their most primal animal instincts. This menagerie of mysterious creatures may manifest themselves in various ways. Some may seem monstrous, while others may seem insignificant, yet each has a valuable lesson to teach. The creatures of The Bestiary represent wild and instinctive forces that surround us and reside within our hearts. Some may symbolize spirit totems that we associate with in an emotional way. By heeding the guidance of The Bestiary, we realize how to focus our own inner strengths.

THE BLACK CAT

YOUR LUCK WILL SOON CHANGE

The Black Cat

An Egyptian hieroglyph depicts a sacred temple cat surrounded by mystical inscriptions. The scarab amulet on its feline chest is a charm of good fortune, designating The Black Cat as a bringer of luck. The ancient Egyptians revered cats and domesticated them from wild animals to become loving companions. In this regard, The Black Cat symbolizes a relationship that has been nurtured over a lengthy period of time. It may also personify someone who is wild at heart, yet conducts themself with decorum.

The Black Cat is a sign that your luck will soon change. The superstitious belief that a black cat crossing your path will alter your luck is commonly associated with a change for the worse, however the appearance of The Black Cat may also end a streak of misfortune. The Black Cat may also represent a superstitious notion that may keep you from progressing in your desired direction in life. If you are heading into dangerous or unfamiliar territory, The Black Cat acts as a warning to avoid unnecessary risks.

Enigmatic and aloof, The Black Cat is temperamental with its affections. This instinctive and intuitive creature is a good judge of human nature and only feels comfortable around those it deems worthy of its love and respect. The Black Cat is a symbol of superstition, secrets and intrigue. Often associated with witchcraft, black cats were believed to be magical and mysterious creatures that strengthened a witch's powers. In this regard, The Black Cat symbolizes secret knowledge and empowerment. Now is the time to channel your energy to develop hidden talents.

THE CHIMERA

IMAGINATION CLOUDS YOUR JUDGEMENT

The Chimera

With the head and upper body of a lion, the legs of a goat and a serpent for a tail, The Chimera represents an unlikely mixture of ideas. This mythical beast symbolizes one who is highly imaginative but prone to flights of fancy, warning that your current pursuits may be unrealistic. Reevaluate your situation and combine your various resources in an innovative way to achieve your desired goal.

The Chimera represents rampant imagination and wild creativity. A healthy imagination stimulates creative thinking, however an overactive imagination may cloud your judgment. An abundance of ideas may obscure your decision process. Combine your varied interests and personal strengths to showcase your best assets. Lofty aspirations require a great deal of imaginative thought and dedication. Thinking outside the box will allow you to achieve seemingly impossible rewards. Visualize a positive outcome and remain focused on your desired goal. An original mixture of styles will lead to something truly unique if you coordinate your ideas in a creative way.

The Chimera embodies free thinking and non-conformity. Stimulate passions by breaking away from the norm and mixing things up. Variety is the spice of life. Seek inspiration from a wide array of sources and defy convention by making a bold statement. The Chimera reminds us that we are all unique combinations of our collected interests. Stay true to yourself and be original.

THE DRAGON

STRENGTH AND WISDOM

The Dragon

The Dragon reigns supreme over the creatures of The Bestiary and has commanding influence over all in his domain. Though mainly regarded as a fearsome monster, The Dragon is also a wise and mystical creature that inspires awe and respect. The Dragon's mere presence symbolizes an intimidating show of force. Though it is fearless and fierce, The Dragon advises to temper your actions with wisdom. Strong words and direct confrontation usually garner desired results without resorting to aggressive action.

A symbol of extreme power, The Dragon represents great strength, wisdom and wealth. Dragons of legend amassed and guarded magnificent treasures and those who foolishly ventured into the dragon's lair intending to plunder its riches met terrible fates. The Dragon warns of dire consequences for seeking personal enrichment through unethical means. Claim only the accolades you rightfully deserve and you will be justly rewarded.

The Dragon spends much of its time hidden in shadows, only venturing from its lair when necessary. It is a slumbering giant that may become an overwhelming force when provoked. As the proverb states, it is best to let sleeping dragons lie. The Dragon may also symbolize an imposing challenge or formidable adversary that, once confronted, cannot be vanquished through conventional means. Engaging in battle with such a foe will have devastating results. Be prepared to relinquish your fight, but if you are forced to take aggressive action, utilize all your power and resources. The Dragon's mighty wings enable it to defy the wind, allowing it to take to flight and soar through the heavens, showing that lofty goals may be achieved by developing your natural abilities and being persistent. Spread your wings and reach for the sky.

THE GRYPHON

**HONOR AND
GOOD LUCK**

The Gryphon

The Gryphon is fierce and magnificent creature from ancient mythology with the body of a lion and the head, wings and talons of an eagle. According to legend, gryphons had a fondness for gold and precious gems and their nests were rumored to hold rare and valuable treasures. Gryphon feathers were highly sought after to make good luck charms that were believed to bring swift resolve to any and all problems.

The Gryphon is a herald of good fortune and signifies that luck is on your side. Taking chances will be profitable at this time. A risk will reap rewards. The Gryphon also represents honor and dignity. If you are at a crossroads, The Gryphon advises to take the most honorable path. Lofty ideals and high expectations are indicative of the demanding nature of this beast. The Gryphon inspires us to work harder, reach higher, and put forth our best effort to produce our finest work.

The Gryphon has great depth of vision and can see all things with vivid clarity. In this regard, The Gryphon represents a true friend who looks out for your best interests and is always by your side in your time of need. Gryphons were said to mate for life, thus they are also a symbol of fidelity and undying loyalty. Be selective when choosing friends or a partner for a relationship, and only trust those you can always rely upon. Reciprocate loyalty with the same to solidify a lasting bond.

THE RAVEN

DARKNESS LOOMS ON THE HORIZON

The Raven

A large raven perched atop a weathered human skull cries a warning to beware forthcoming darkness. The Raven is an ominous messenger that warns that dark times lie ahead. Those who take comfort in the shadows may welcome the approaching darkness as a time when they will be at home in their natural element. In this regard, The Raven advises to explore the mysteries of the night and embrace the dark.

The Raven crosses between the spirit realm and the realm of the living, delivering news of grave concern. This dark harbinger is a creature of the shadows and a scavenger among the ruins. As a carrion bird, The Raven seeks things that have been discarded or overlooked by others and uses them to its advantage. In this regard, The Raven exemplifies the adage of "waste not, want not," and advises to utilize every bit of useful material at your disposal to attain your desires.

Though associated with danger and woe, The Raven does not necessarily represent imminent misfortune. The Raven warns that darkness looms on the horizon and advises to take heed. The Raven's presence is a sign that circumstances may worsen, however any damage caused by this forthcoming turmoil may be avoidable with proper preparation. Do not ignore the warning signs of a potential problem. Prepare for all possibilities and brace yourself to weather the coming storm.

THE SERPENT

A SLY AND SUBTLE APPROACH IS NEEDED

The Serpent

The Serpent represents one who is sly and devious and advises to be wary of hidden agendas and half-truths. The Serpent exudes a hypnotic grace that may appear charming, but it is a dangerous predator that should be treated with caution and avoided whenever possible. Whereas some serpents strike swiftly, delivering venomous bites, others slowly constrict your freedom until you succumb to them. Likewise, The Serpent may also constrict your thinking, stifling your creative ideas in order to make your thoughts in tune with its own narrow vision.

The Serpent watches and plans from a safe distance, remaining concealed in plain sight. The Serpent may represent a secret admirer who keeps their true desires hidden, or one who covets from afar. The Serpent sheds its outer skin once it has outgrown it. In this regard, The Serpent represents a shedding of old habits and a physical or aesthetic renewal. Discard unwanted baggage that impedes your progress and holds you in the past.

Stealthy, cunning and deceptive, The Serpent may go completely unnoticed while waiting for the opportune time to strike. The Serpent advises to be patient, keep a low profile and wait for the right time make your move. Do not announce your plans before you are ready to act upon them. Use the element of surprise to your full advantage. A sly and subtle approach is needed to achieve a current goal.

THE SPIDER

BE METICULOUS AND PATIENT

The Spider

The Spider symbolizes diligence and industrious activity, but also advocates patience and discretion. The Spider's meticulous work while weaving its web shows us how success favors the prepared and that persistence yields captivating results. Planning and diligent work will allow you to attain your desires and reap great rewards. Put maximum effort into preparation then bide your time for the optimum moment to spring into action. Good things come to those who wait.

The Spider can bridge immense gaps and distances through relentless, persistent effort. In addition, The Spider shows us how common threads can unite opposing viewpoints. The Spider's many legs work together with meticulous precision to build its web, symbolizing the interweaving of ideas to create a unified plan.

The Spider's web is a marvel of craftsmanship that is both beautiful and functional. Coordinate your ideas to create a comfortable environment that is aesthetically pleasing and serves a practical purpose. The proper workspace will enable you to be more efficient and productive.

The Spider is a diminutive and fragile creature that can escape notice in most situations, but it is also a highly proficient predator, capable of overcoming difficult challenges and vanquishing much larger foes. The Spider reminds us to pay close attention to the small details. Don't underestimate the importance of things that may seem insignificant. Take the time to secure all loose ends to ensure success in your current endeavors.

THE UNICORN

GOOD FORTUNE AND FRIENDSHIP

The Unicorn

The Unicorn is a sign of good things to come. This fabled creature represents imminent good fortune and success in current endeavors. Its appearance is an omen that you will be rewarded by fate. The Unicorn symbolizes a rare and enchanting breed. Embrace that which makes you unique in order to capitalize on your special abilities and personal strengths. Be confident with the knowledge that positive things are on the horizon.

The Unicorn is also a symbol of healing and potent sexuality. According to ancient lore, a unicorn's horn was believed to hold powerful magic and was used in charms and spells to grant sexual prowess and fertility. Your powers of attraction are heightened. Your love life flourishes as romance thrives. The Unicorn's energy is also associated with good health and is a sign that a healing process will have a positive outcome. A recovery may take time in order to heal properly and fully.

The Unicorn may also represent a rare find or a coveted yet elusive prize that seems unattainable. According to legend, only someone pure of heart can comfort and tame this wild and magical beast, however, once a unicorn bonds with someone, it remains a faithful companion. In this regard, The Unicorn symbolizes a true friend. Compassion and trust form the basis for a loyal friendship. Kindness reaps valuable rewards.

THE WOLF

BEWARE WHO YOU TRUST

The Wolf

A relentless hunter, The Wolf is both feared and respected. This wild beast is selective yet extremely loyal in matters of friendship and family. The Wolf functions best within its pack, exemplifying that more can be accomplished together with a like-minded group than one can achieve alone. Scrutinize your friends and associates to ensure they are trustworthy before confiding in them or delegating any responsibilities to them. Be a contributing team player and work together with others to achieve a mutual goal.

The Wolf advises to be careful who you trust. The saying "beware a wolf in sheep's clothing," delivers a warning to watch out for those who try to appear harmless as a deceptive ruse to get close to you, only to prosper at your expense. Someone who sees you as easy prey may harbor harmful intentions. Be wary of strangers who may attempt to deceive you in order to gain your confidence.

The Wolf is primarily a nocturnal creature and is thus more comfortable beneath the cover of darkness. In this regard, it may signify that nighttime activity will yield desirable results or warn that a hidden danger lurks in the shadows.

The savage nature of The Wolf exemplifies following one's natural instincts. The Wolf's mindset is based solely on primal emotions. The Wolf wastes no time on the nuances of tact or etiquette when in pursuit of its desires. This bold creature strikes swiftly as it closes in on its quarry. Now is the time for fast action. Heed your instincts.

THE WYVERN

YOUR SECRETS ARE SAFE

The Wyvern

The Wyvern is a keeper of secrets and granter of second chances. It is a sign that hidden things remain safe and secure. The Wyvern advises to keep your ideas to yourself at this time. The best kept secrets are never shared. Don't reveal your intentions until you are ready to fully enact them. Likewise, don't betray a confidence that has been entrusted to you.

The Wyvern may also represent a conflict of emotions or feelings of guilt. Now is the time to forgive past transgressions and free yourself from any lingering ghosts that persist to haunt you. Learn from experience and mistakes of the past and pursue your goals with newfound wisdom. Failure teaches valuable lessons. Fate grants you the opportunity to redeem yourself. Do not repeat old mistakes. Capitalize on opportunities that allow you to correct past regrets.

Because of its fearless nature, The Wyvern often appears in heraldry as a symbol of courage and strength. A kindred spirit of The Dragon and The Gryphon, The Wyvern shares their ability to take to flight in order to reach lofty goals. If you fall short of attaining your desires, analyze your mistakes and prepare a better strategy for the future. Be ready when fate presents a second opportunity that may allow you to achieve your dreams.

THE TREASURY

The Treasury consists of 12 cards that represent valuable, mystical artifacts that will aid you in the attainment of your goals and prepare you in fulfilling your true destiny. The relics of The Treasury are symbolic markers that guide you along your life's path, helping you to choose which direction to pursue at specific junctures. The Treasury reveals the unseen forces that surround your daily life as well as mystical powers that may be at work on your behalf. By becoming familiar with the gifts of The Treasury, you may come to fully understand the outside energies affecting a current situation and realize how to best utilize the resources at your disposal.

THE CADUCEUS

YOU WILL RECEIVE
NEWS FROM AFAR

The Caduceus

The snake-entwined staff of the Greek god Hermes, The Caduceus is the symbol of the messenger and sign of the healer. It is an omen that announces the arrival of news from afar. The ramifications of an important message should be taken to heart. The winged Caduceus represents swift and deliberate action. Don't delay your current endeavors. Hesitation leads to missed opportunities. Act now and work quickly to capitalize on the circumstances of the moment.

The Caduceus signifies good health and a swift healing process. Pursuing a healthy diet and engaging in exercise will allow you to look and feel your best and enable you to enjoy life to the fullest. The Caduceus is a sign that a recovery process is underway. Now is the time to mend old wounds. Relaxation and rest will help with recuperation.

The Caduceus was believed to be capable of inducing sleep and awakening people from deathly slumber. Engage in adventurous new activities to end a period of listlessness. This may imply visiting an unexplored destination or simply taking a trip for the sake of making new discoveries along your journey.

The Caduceus is also a symbol of merchants and commerce, designating success in matters of money and trade. Look beyond face value to assess true worth and use your negotiating skills to broker the best deal possible. Creative bargaining will garner a favorable outcome. Marketing your talents to their fullest potential will allow you to reap great rewards.

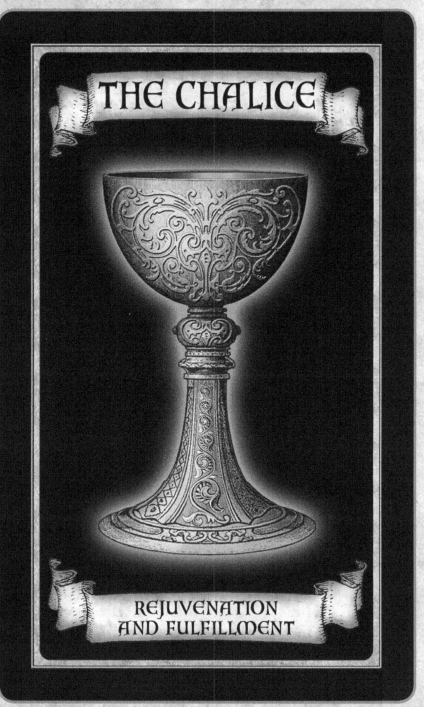

THE CHALICE

REJUVENATION AND FULFILLMENT

The Chalice

The Chalice is the symbol of rejuvenation, fulfillment and abundance, designating a period of good health and physical prosperity. The Chalice imparts healing energy that replenishes physical and emotional strength, invigorating both body and spirit. The Chalice symbolizes a stimulating impetus that restores youthful exuberance and rejuvenates us when we lose momentum.

The Grail of the Crusades was a legendary chalice that inspired countless quests and adventures in unknown lands. Sought by many but held by few, The Chalice is a rare and valuable find that eludes all but the most determined. It is a treasure of unequaled value that holds great mystical power. In this regard, The Chalice symbolizes the prize at the end of a quest or the realization of a dream. A lifelong goal is within your reach. Replenish your resources and resume your quest with a newfound vigor.

Used in arcane rituals, The Chalice grants spiritual energy to those who partake of its contents. Among its many powers, it is believed to allow the living to commune with the spirit realm. Your senses are in tune with the otherworldly. Higher powers heed your summons. The Chalice also represents attainment and accomplishment, signifying wishes granted and promises kept. Those who partake of The Chalice will be rewarded with plenitude and abundance. You will be bestowed with bountiful good fortune. Share your blessings with others.

THE DAGGER

CONFLICT AND DANGER LIE IN WAIT

The Dagger

The Dagger is a symbol of danger, conflict and adversity, signifying that trying times loom on the horizon. This may manifest as a strong clash of opinions or possibly a physical confrontation. Don't allow a minor conflict or argument to evolve into a serious fight. Disarm the situation before it escalates to something more severe.

The Dagger is also a symbol of loss and physical harm that warns to be on your guard. Beware of back-stabbers and thieves. Protect yourself by heightening your awareness of possible threats. Be alert to things happening behind your back and be ready to defend yourself and safeguard your belongings.

The Dagger can be either a creative or destructive force, depending on the intent of its bearer. The Dagger can deal a minor cut or a deep, piercing stab that may be fatal. Use your strengths in proper measure to achieve the precise results you desire. Don't waste time with unnecessary formalities surrounding a fleeting opportunity. Cut to the heart of the matter. The Dagger is easily concealed, allowing you to keep your most powerful asset hidden, yet close at hand. Don't reveal your secret strengths until you need to use them.

The Dagger foretells that a new venture will require little effort if you hone your skills and utilize them to your best advantage. The Dagger is also an instrument of severance. In this regard, The Dagger signifies a time to cut ties with things that are holding you back. Free yourself of excess baggage that has no use or worth. Make a clean cut from the past.

THE GATE

A BARRIER KEEPS YOU FROM YOUR GOAL

The Gate

The Gate represents an unavoidable obstacle that stands between you and your goal. Although it may act as an impenetrable barrier, it is easily opened by those who possess the proper key, granting access to that which lies beyond. This may manifest as a difficult challenge that will require a specific set of skills to overcome. Analyze that which is holding you back and determine an exact solution to your situation. You may not possess all you require to advance your position at this time. Seek whatever key ingredient that may be missing.

The Gate stands at the threshold of unexplored territory. This landmark may represent the end of a current phase in your life or the beginning of promising new era. Though The Gate restricts certain freedoms, it also grants security, thwarting outsiders from crossing personal boundaries. The Gate allows you to admit those you desire into your domain, while stopping others from invading your privacy. The Gate maintains a personal perimeter and secures things from running wild, allowing you to keep your affairs concealed and controlled.

The Gate is not a permanent obstacle. It is a controlled barrier that may be unlocked at any given time by those who use the appropriate key. The Gate is an artistically ornate and structurally solid barrier, designed to thwart admission to restricted areas, yet allowing a glimpse at what lies beyond. In this regard, The Gate represents a portal to aspirations and dreams, for once it has been unlocked, it provides a means to attain that which you truly desire.

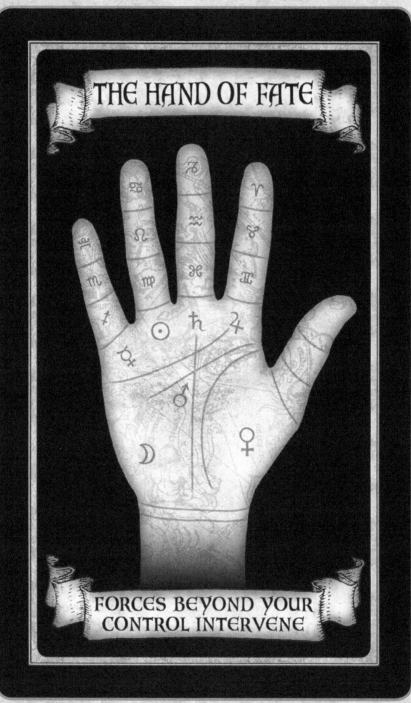

THE HAND OF FATE

FORCES BEYOND YOUR
CONTROL INTERVENE

The Hand of Fate

The Hand of Fate is an unpredictable and mysterious force that intercedes in human affairs from time to time, affecting one's destiny at important junctures in their life. It is a righteous power that acts to maintain balance and harmony among all living things. The Hand of Fate is a sign that justice will prevail, allowing universal powers to bestow fitting consequences for a person's actions. The Hand of Fate rises to dispense poetic justice, deservedly punishing bad deeds and rewarding benevolent acts. It may manifest as a serendipitous gift for those who strive to do good, or as a justly reprimanding force for those who cause or intend harm.

The art of Palmistry reveals an individual's personal destiny by reading the secrets etched in flesh. All signs of the Zodiac are represented here, thus The Hand of Fate holds the destinies of all living things. The Hand of Fate intervenes in difficult situations at life's most trying times, bringing people together with opportunity and directing paths to cross for mutually beneficial results. The Hand of Fate may also represent a person's destined calling, delivering a message that you are exactly where you need to be at this point in your life.

The Hand of Fate signifies an intervention of outside forces beyond human control that sway and guide you along your destined path. Heed subtle signs and fate will direct you along the proper course. At times, The Hand of Fate may disrupt or hinder your current plans, causing a necessary delay or forcing a complete change of course along a more prosperous path. Strive to put forth your best effort in a current endeavor and know that fate will determine the most befitting outcome for you. If something was meant to be, The Hand of Fate will make it so.

THE HOURGLASS

TIME IS OF THE ESSENCE

The Hourglass

As the sands of the hourglass slip away, they remind us that time is fleeting and of the essence. Be careful not to procrastinate or you may miss an important window of opportunity. Take the initiative to act before it's too late. Perfect timing will play an important factor in a current endeavor. Be aware of your time constraints and strive to meet all deadlines. You can accomplish a great deal more if you manage your time properly.

The Hourglass serves as a reminder that our time on earth is limited. Make the most of every day and don't fall into an unproductive pattern of activity. Spend time doing the things you truly love, surrounded by those closest to your heart. The Hourglass may represent a need to prioritize your time to deal with urgent matters. Designate time for work and leisure to create a harmonious balance in your life.

A symbol of synchronicity, The Hourglass is a sign that your actions are in tune with the universal forces that surround you. You are exactly where you were meant to be at this time in your life. Staying true to your current path will lead you to your desired goal if you use your time wisely. The Hourglass reminds us that time is constantly moving forward and cannot be reversed. Reflect upon the past, but don't dwell there. Time is precious and we never know what tomorrow may bring. Strive to make every moment count and live your life to its absolute fullest.

THE KEY

LOCKED DOORS CAN NOW BE OPENED

The Key

You possess the ability to resolve a current dilemma or bypass any obstacle. Locked doors can now be opened and hidden secrets may now be revealed. The Key enables you to achieve things that were previously beyond your reach, allowing you to realize your greatest aspirations and dreams.

The Key is also a symbol of trust and responsibility. Do not abuse the confidence that another has placed in you. The Key unlocks secret knowledge and grants permission to forbidden realms. In some instances, you may be the key to resolving a problem for someone close to you. The Key is the result of meticulous craftsmanship to create the solution for one specific obstacle. In this regard, The Key represents a perfect fit in a relationship, as well as a precise solution to clearing a blocked path.

The Key may represent a physical object or specific knowledge that allows you to unlock unsolved mysteries or overcome a current issue that thwarts forward progress along your desired path. Knowledge, wisdom and persistence are all keys to achieving your goals.

Those who possess The Key hold the power to attain things that are beyond the reach of others. The Key will transform followers into leaders and will allow outsiders to enter the inner circle. Once a barrier has been opened, do not close it behind you. Use The Key wisely to unlock a brighter future and allow others to reap the benefits of your abilities and success.

LOVE

TRUE LOVE AND FIDELITY

Love

Winged Cupid with bow and arrows in hand stands atop a golden heart, symbolizing true love and romance. Love represents honesty, fidelity, a lasting union, and a rekindling of affections. It is a sign that you will attain your heart's desire and that the love you give is faithfully and sincerely reciprocated. Love may manifest in a variety of unpredictable ways. Keep an open mind to romantic possibilities. A current friendship may blossom into something deeper and more passionate.

The heart is the physical vessel from which our life's essence flows. It is the artistic representation of our emotional center. Though the love it holds inspires and empowers us to achieve great things, it is a fragile treasure. A broken heart can cause a sadness that is more painful than any physical injury. A heart of gold symbolizes a person who is extraordinarily caring and giving of themselves. Opening your heart to others will grant you emotional rewards.

Love is a sign that your attractive and endearing qualities are at their peak. True love goes beyond physical passion. It is a deep bond between two people who share a romantic attraction as well as a mutual respect and a selfless, unconditional acceptance of one another. Love guides our heartfelt emotions, and advises compassion when dealing with others.

Love heals all wounds and emotional scars. It can soothe the pain caused by loss or hardship and can inspire passionate works of art, literature and music. Follow your heart to pursue that which you truly love and you will realize your dreams.

THE MYSTIC CIRCLE

YOUR ABILITIES WILL BE ENHANCED

The Mystic Circle

A ring of ancient runes surrounds a central circle of three dragons, representing past, present and future. The encompassing runic symbols hold the arcane power of the ages for those who have the ability to harness their energies. The Mystic Circle radiates vibrant magic that invigorates hidden inner strengths and safeguards those who draw upon its power. This ancient talisman symbolizes meditation and introspection, advising you to look within, not without, for the solution to a current dilemma.

The Mystic Circle represents spiritual and occult beliefs and the empowering magic of The Old Ways. While within The Mystic Circle, your natural abilities will be augmented. Focus your energy on your main goal and pursue it with renewed vigor.

The Mystic Circle enhances arcane powers and allows you to become more attuned to the unseen realm. Your extra-sensory perceptions are heightened. Follow your intuition and listen to your inner voice. Heed prophetic messages in dreams and be aware of any spiritual signs that might guide your path.

The Mystic Circle also offers protection to all within its confines. Those who mean you harm will be powerless against you as long as you remain where you are and stand firm in your beliefs. The Mystic Circle reinforces confidence and a sense of security, but also emboldens assertive action. Your powers of persuasion are at their peak potential. Remain determined and be confident in your abilities and you will be destined to succeed.

THE ORACLE

SEEK WISDOM AND GUIDANCE FROM ELDERS

The Oracle

Winged deities and an all-seeing eye comprise a symbolic motif depicting the temple of ancient wisdom and divine truth. The Oracle is the venerable keeper of the compiled knowledge of the ages. This enigmatic guide advises to seek the wisdom of elders. Consult books, teachers or knowledgeable authorities to acquire the information needed to attain your goals. The Oracle may also represent a sacrifice made in the quest for enlightenment. Decide what is most important to you and focus your thoughts and energy on attaining it. Once the path is clear, do not stray from it.

The Oracle symbolizes the compilation of knowledge and wisdom gleaned from the past. Ask the advice of an expert and seek guidance from those with relevant experience. The Oracle may communicate through spiritual means as well. Look for the hidden meaning in dreams and heed prophetic signs. The Oracle delivers a message of resolute truth, which is sometimes harsh in its honesty. Heed constructive criticism and thoughtful suggestions to improve your current situation.

The Oracle also advises to use your experience to teach others. Share your knowledge with those who could best benefit from your expertise. There is no greater reward than the feeling of satisfaction from helping others. When interpreted correctly, The Oracle's message can reveal future landmarks and guide you toward your ultimate destiny. Listen closely and heed sage advice.

THE SHIELD

YOU ARE SAFE FROM HARM

The Shield

The Shield designates a barrier that protects you from harmful intent. While holding The Shield, your adversaries cannot penetrate your defenses. Do not allow harsh words or negative comments to affect you. A thick skin will keep you safe from harm. The Shield reminds us that an important strategy in any battle is maintaining a solid defense. Compile and fortify your ideas before engaging in conflict and keep your guard up at all times while traversing potentially dangerous territory.

The Shield may also represent an emotional barrier, advising you to guard your true feelings until trust is gained. Discretion is the better part of valor. Once you become comfortable in a situation, The Shield can be lowered to allow a free exchange of thoughts and emotions. If The Shield is wielded by another, you may have to disarm your words or actions in order to get your opponent to lower their natural defenses.

The Phoenix emblazoned upon The Shield signifies a warrior spirit that has risen from the ashes to emerge stronger than before. Bearing this mythical icon, The Shield also represents one who has learned from past experience and grown wiser and stronger. Take lessons from past mistakes and be careful not to repeat them. The Shield advises to be fully prepared to meet any and all impending threats. Leave nothing to chance and proceed with caution when entering risky situations.

THE TALISMAN

YOU ARE DESTINED TO SUCCEED

The Talisman

The Talisman is a keepsake or charm that has deep significance and grants luck to those who carry it. Good fortune shines upon you and you are destined to succeed in your current pursuits. The Talisman is a vessel that has been imbued with mystical power through magical means. Often inscribed with arcane symbols, The Talisman bestows its bearer with enhanced perceptions that enlighten the senses beyond the mortal scope, granting them insights into the spirit realm.

A cherished treasure with deep personal meaning, The Talisman provides security and emotional support, bolsters confidence and empowers your natural abilities and latent skills. The Talisman is not a mere trinket that may be bought or sold. In order to preserve its energy, a talisman must be given freely as a gift and may only be passed on to someone truly deserving.

The power of The Talisman is amplified by the strength of its bearer, and weakened by a lack of faith in one's own abilities. Believe in yourself and you will succeed. Focus your mind to channel your energy to attain your desires.

The Talisman also acts as a ward against misfortune. In this regard, The Talisman advises against any potentially risky or dangerous actions that may pose a threat, however it can also act as a reassuring shield, bolstering confidence at times when you are required to venture outside of your personal comfort zone. The Talisman's mystical qualities exude a positive energy that aid in the attainment of any goal. Beneath the power of The Talisman, success is well within your reach.

THE ELEMENTS

The Elements consist of 8 cards depicting the celestial bodies and various forces of nature that surround and influence us every day. The Elements are ever-present and exert specific energies that empower us in several different ways. The Elements represent the uncontrollable forces of the universe that affect humanity. By understanding the influences and effects of The Elements, we can learn how to attune ourselves to universal forces and anticipate many of the unknown factors that may arise along our life's path.

THE SUN

YOUR PERSEVERANCE IS REWARDED

The Sun

The Sun casts its light on the world, illuminating the darkness and enabling us to see all things clearly. A period of enlightenment will allow you to discover secrets hidden in the shadows. The Sun also symbolizes one who is the center of attention, whom all things revolve around. Beneath The Sun's radiant light, you will gain recognition and acclaim. A perpetual source of energy, The Sun grants illumination and warmth to all who partake of its radiance. An energetic and warm disposition will endear you to those you meet. Strive to shine your brightest.

The Sun is depicted above a winged scarab beetle, representing the ancient Egyptian god, Ra, who was believed to move the sun across the heavens each day. In this regard, The Sun symbolizes unrelenting effort focused on one specific goal and foretells that your perseverance will be rewarded. Strive to be continually reliable and productive. Though The Sun's radiant glow offers enlightenment, staring directly into its fiery brilliance can be blinding. Do not indulge in excess. Too much of a good thing can have detrimental consequences.

Though The Sun shines brightest when directly overhead, it is the most beautiful at dawn and dusk. The dawning sun represents new ideas, unexplored realms and bright prospects on the horizon, while the setting sun represents the end of a current phase and ideas that have run their course. The cycle repeats itself endlessly, showing how as one venture fades into the horizon, new possibilities soon arise. Do not allow yourself to get discouraged by unfulfilled dreams of the past. The future holds brighter things.

THE MOON

YOU WILL BE GUIDED
THROUGH DARKNESS

The Moon

A glowing crescent hovers above two ancient Egyptian gods—Anubis, guide of the underworld, and Khonsu, lord of the moon. A beacon in the black of night, The Moon guides those who are lost in darkness. The Moon represents illumination and discovery, shining through the pervading gloom to reveal things that are concealed and enabling us to clearly see our chosen path. If you are struggling to find your way, seek guidance from one who can assess your current situation from a higher perspective.

The Moon's various phases represent constant change, symbolizing versatility in outlook and demeanor. Don't get locked into one specific mindset or style. The gravitational pull of the moon controls the ocean tides, thus it has a marked effect on earthly matters. In this regard, The Moon represents an inexplicable yet undeniable attraction that spans a great distance. Be aware that your actions may be subtly swayed from afar, and that you may exert influence over a distant situation as well.

The Moon's light has serene, soothing qualities and thus represents tranquility and a time of peace. Relaxation through meditative introspection will relieve stress and attune your mind and body. The Moon possesses an enigmatic dual nature, for while it shines bright in the night sky, it also has a secretive, hidden dark side. Be aware that someone who appears charming on the surface may harbor dark secrets. The unseen shadows of The Moon hold unfathomable mysteries, advising to keep your intimate thoughts and feelings concealed. An air of mystique will enhance your allure.

THE STARS

A LONG JOURNEY BRINGS REWARDS

The Stars

The Stars guide us through trying times, providing direction to those who are aimless or lost. The Stars can be used to find your bearings and navigate vast distances. Analyze all pertinent facts surrounding your current situation and plot the most direct course to reach your goal. The Stars form the constellations of the Zodiac, designating our astrological signs. In this regard, The Stars set our destinies in motion and advise us along the best paths throughout our lives.

The Stars represent a voyage that spans a great distance. They may also indicate a separation or a possible reunion. Reach out to old relations you may have lost touch with. Plan a trip to a destination that intrigues you. A journey brings rewards. The Stars fill the vastness of space with the promise of endless, unexplored possibilities. Though they lie beyond our reach, they stimulate our imaginations, inspiring us to dream and reach further as we pursue aspirations and ideas that transcend the mundane.

Casting a wish upon a star is believed to make your wish come true. Your dream will become reality if you focus your thoughts and efforts on it. The Stars also symbolize the people in your life that you hold in the highest esteem. Take lessons from those that you most respect and admire. Heed their guidance and follow the paths they pursued to achieve their lofty goals. Never lose sight of your inspiration or dreams. When The Stars align, all things are possible.

AIR

LIBRA GEMINI AQUARIUS

SEEK A UNION OF
MIND AND SPIRIT

AIR

Air is the element of mind and spirit, and represents the unseen forces of nature. Air manifests itself in those who are lighthearted and free-spirited, however, a dreamy, indecisive and forgetful nature may be attributed to Air as well. The signs of the Zodiac that are governed by Air are Aquarius, Gemini and Libra. Air advises to seek guidance in the spiritual, ethereal and philosophical realms.

Though unseen, Air is a vital component to all life. In this regard, Air represents the invisible forces that surround us daily to influence and nurture us. Air provides the open forum to hold ideas aloft and manifests as intellectual thought and analytical reflection. Because it allows unrestricted movement, Air symbolizes complete freedom of choice and expression. Don't let anything hold you back from being the person you truly want to be. After contemplating the facts of a situation, speak your mind and share your opinions openly.

Air is an essential ingredient of fire, making it burn hotter and brighter under the right circumstances. Air may ignite if a combustible situation is sparked, but the removal of air will snuff the flames and extinguish the fire. In this regard, Air and Fire are kindred elements that naturally coexist. Air represents a union of mind and soul, emphasizing a balance of free-thinking and philosophical belief. Those influenced by Air should strive to keep an open mind and seek the company of intellectual and spiritual equals.

EARTH

CAPRICORN
TAURUS
VIRGO

UTILIZE LOGIC, REASON
AND COMMON SENSE

Earth

Earth is the element of logic and reason, and represents the passive forces of nature. The influences of Earth may be found in those who are grounded, dependable and organized. The signs of the Zodiac that are governed by Earth are Capricorn, Taurus and Virgo. Earth advises to be practical and use common sense, and also advocates being resolute and standing firm in your convictions.

Earth can be molded, sculpted and shaped into works of art and may also be used to create the building blocks of towering structures, allowing us to transform our dreams and ideas into tangible reality. Earth creates a stable platform to build upon, exemplifying how a strong foundation is the basis of a solid and lasting relationship. Monuments sculpted from earthen stone stand as a testament to past achievements and promises etched in stone endure the test of time, retaining their message even as they are subjected to the extreme forces of nature.

Earth holds vital nutrients that feed and nurture plant life, in addition to concealing treasures, such as gold, silver and precious jewels. Look below the surface to find the hidden merits of a situation that may seem unappealing at the ground level. You may have to dig deep to discover the true value of a project or relationship. Mindful prospecting will uncover profitable rewards. Earth manifests as a sensible and reliable friend who offers stability, lending support when spirits are low. Take time to appreciate life's simple pleasures.

FIRE

RECKLESS ACTIONS
LEAD TO CONFLICT

Fire

Fire is the element of action and energy, and represents the destructive forces of nature. Fire manifests itself in those who are passionate and aggressive. The signs of the Zodiac that are governed by Fire are Aries, Leo and Sagittarius. Fire advocates spontaneity and encourages acting on impulse rather than engaging in thoughtful planning and preparation. Don't waste time pondering all of your options. Boldly leap into life.

Fire may also manifest as the flames of desire, indicating a burning passion that has been stoked. Focus your intense emotions to allow your inner fire to burn brighter. Be wary that a small spark may set off a major disruption or conflict. Letting your passions run wild may result in irreparable damage. Avoid combustible situations and do not fan the flames of rage. Be prepared to leave a situation if it begins to burn out of control. Wildfire poses a threat until it has been completely extinguished.

When properly harnessed, Fire is a source of great power that can be used to generate heat and energy, but when not contained or controlled, it can be a fierce and destructive force. When dealing with Fire, the risk of getting burned is always present. Proceed with caution when entering a new venture.

Fire mixes best with Air and other Fire signs, although a clash of two fiery personalities can have volatile results. A raging Fire consumes everything in its path, leaving nothing but ashes and ruins in its wake. In this regard, the first signs of Fire should be closely heeded. Act quickly to quell a heated situation.

WATER

SCORPIO

PISCES

CANCER

EMOTIONS ARE
AT THEIR PEAK

WATER

Water is the element of change and emotion, and represents the nurturing forces of nature. The influences of Water may be found in those who are caring and persistent, although they may be temperamental at times. The signs of the Zodiac that are governed by Water are Cancer, Pisces and Scorpio. Water indicates a time when emotions are at their peak, reminding us to be sensitive to the needs of others.

Appearing in several forms in nature, Water is the most versatile of the elements. Be prepared to adapt to a changing environment. Gentle rains bring vital nourishment, however violent downpours and raging flood waters can cause great destruction. Water is essential to life, however in extreme conditions, it can drown aspirations. Take things in moderation and allow fate to follow its natural course.

Because Water can extinguish fire, it represents the soothing effects of a tranquil demeanor. Strive to remain calm in the face of heated conflict. Considerate words and gestures will soothe rising tempers to prevail over anger. Running Water can wear away the hardest stone over time, eroding mountains and creating canyons through rocky terrain. By being unrelenting and persistent, you can wear others down and bring them around to your way of thinking. Make your own way and stay the course and you will persevere in the long run.

WINDS OF CHANGE

YOUR SURROUNDINGS WILL UNDERGO TRANSITION

The Winds of Change

The Winds of Change foretell of a shift in your current circumstances that may potentially alter your destiny. You must decide whether to stay your course or adapt your current direction to flow with the changes. New prospects and potential new problems loom on the horizon. Brace yourself for the possibility of a forthcoming tempest and be prepared for alterations in your surroundings that may deeply affect your life.

The Winds of Change compel us to leave our personal comfort zones. At times, this forced change is necessary to help us grow. What may originally be perceived as upheaval to our lives may actually be the impetus that sets us down a more prosperous path. The Winds of Change may bring an end to a stifled relationship, or cause you to pursue a more rewarding career. The Winds of Change will compel you to evaluate your current situation to discover what matters most in your life, urging you to decide what direction you truly wish to pursue.

Those who go against the winds will face resistance, and though their journey may be more difficult, they will inevitably go wherever they choose in life. Those who allow the winds to guide them will have smooth sailing but will not have the freedom to decide their own course. The choice is yours as to whether you will defy or surrender to the winds. You must decide if you are a relentless pioneer who works diligently to blaze your own trail, or a follower who relaxes in the comfort of complacency. There are benefits to both mindsets which can be looked at as pursuing a more fulfilled life versus enjoying a simpler life.

READING
THE CARDS

The various oracles of the cards enable the reader to forecast future events and enlighten the inquirer as to the best path to follow concerning matters of love, money, health and general prosperity, offering insightful advice. A card may represent the person being read, a circumstance, or it may signify an outside influence.

Each card holds a separate and unique meaning and may be referenced individually, as the specific divinatory meanings are plain to interpret. However, if a more in-depth reading is desired, the cards may be interpreted by considering both their general meaning and their relationship to other cards in a given spread.

Allow your intuition to guide you as you interpret the cards. If reading for another person, be sure to keep them actively involved during the reading, asking or answering questions rather than simply observing.

Decide from the following spreads which is most appropriate for the type of question you wish to ask. Shuffle the cards while thinking of the matter in question. Next, cut the deck into three piles. Gather up the piles and begin laying out the cards, one at a time, in the order that they appear in the spread. Make sure the cards are dealt face-down, then after the spread is complete, turn each card over in order.

The Oracle of the Dawning Day

If you want a quick answer to what the future holds, you may rely on a simple one-card reading. Hold the deck in both hands and concentrate upon the question "What will the new day bring?" Shuffle the deck three times, each time asking your question out loud. Lay the cards face down and cut the deck three times. Turn the top card face up to reveal the answer to your question.

The Oracle of Kindred Spirits

This method is used to gauge the compatibility of a relationship between two people, for either love or friendship. The deck must first be shuffled by both people. One person then cuts the deck into two piles and the other person chooses one pile for the reading. Each person in turn asks a question out loud, then draws one card from the chosen pile. Turn over the card to reveal and interpret the answer. Alternate asking questions between both people. No more than three questions may be asked by each person.

Examples of relationship-based questions are:
"What does the future hold for us?"
"Will our relationship be a lasting one?"
"What obstacles might we encounter?"

The Seer's Fan

This spread consists of a five-card fan layout and is used to forecast the future in regard to specific concerns such as matters of Love, Health and Money.

1. Represents you or your present situation.

2. Represents health and physical well-being.

3. Represents love and friendship in your life.

4. Represents an immediate concern. This card is the strongest oracle of future events.

5. Represents spiritual harmony.

6. Represents wealth and material prosperity.

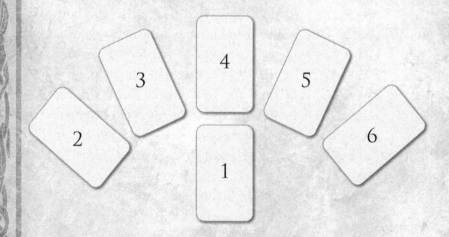

The Oracle of the Four Seasons

This spread may be used to clarify important matters surrounding a present situation. Reflecting on the past is useful in preparing for the future and may be quite helpful in overcoming obstacles which may stand between you and your true destiny.

WINTER symbolizes a time of resolution and represents the distant past.

SPRING symbolizes a time of growth and represents the distant future.

SUMMER symbolizes a time of action and represents the immediate future.

AUTUMN symbolizes a time of reflection and represents the recent past.

1	2	3	4
WINTER	SPRING	SUMMER	AUTUMN

NORTH

WEST

YOU

EAST

SOUTH

The Oracle of the Four Winds

This spread gives insights about the people and mystical forces that surround you. It may be used for determining the past, present and future of the physical and spiritual realms.

Begin by placing the central card, then lay the cards in the following order: North, South, West, East. For the most accurate reading, position yourself to face due North.

THE CENTER card represents you or your present situation.

NORTH—The Oracle of the Spiritual Realm pertains to dreams and intangible ideals, representing that which you aspire to.

SOUTH—The Oracle of the Physical Realm pertains to earthly pursuits and material concerns.

WEST—The Oracle of the Past Realm represents the setting sun or that which has been. This oracle helps us to learn from our mistakes or to avoid repeating negative situations, and is useful in deciphering and interpreting present and future events.

EAST—The Oracle of the Future Realm represents the rising sun or that which is yet to be. This oracle is helpful in preparing oneself for oncoming events which are sometimes avoidable but more often inevitable.

NORTH WEST 6	NORTH 2	NORTH EAST 7
WEST 4	YOU 1	EAST 5
SOUTH WEST 8	SOUTH 3	SOUTH EAST 9

The Oracle of the World

This spread elaborates on the Oracle of the Four Winds by offering further insight into the spiritual and physical realms. Begin by placing the central card, then lay the cards in the following order:

1. **THE CENTER** card represents you or your present situation.

2. **NORTH:** The Oracle of the Spiritual Realm pertains to dreams and intangible ideals, representing that to which you aspire.

3. **SOUTH:** The Oracle of the Physical Realm pertains to earthly pursuits and material concerns.

4. **WEST:** The Oracle of the Past Realm represents the setting sun, or that which has been. This oracle helps us to learn from our mistakes or to avoid repeating negative situations, and is useful in deciphering and interpreting present and future events.

5. **EAST:** The Oracle of the Future Realm represents the rising sun, or that which is yet to be. This oracle is helpful in preparing yourself for oncoming events which are sometimes avoidable, but more often inevitable.

6. **NORTHWEST:** Represents a Past Spiritual or Romantic Influence.

7. **NORTHEAST:** Represents a Future Spiritual or Romantic Influence you will encounter.

8. **SOUTHWEST:** Represents a Past Physical Influence in your life regarding matters of health and money.

9. **SOUTHEAST:** Represents a Future Physical influence you will encounter regarding matters of health and money.

WISDOM OF THE AGES

Throughout the ages, oracles and mystics of every culture foretold future events by various means of divination. These seers mastered the practice of techniques such as astrology, palmistry, phrenology, card reading, pendulums and casting bones. Wise in the ways of the forgotten lore and the enchanted arts, these ancient oracles utilized mystical alphabets, rune magic, love spells and charms, candle magic, alchemy, gemstones and sacred Yantras. It was believed that their vision pierced the mortal veil and enabled them to commune with the spirit realm, granting them otherworldly knowledge of human destiny and allowing them to clearly see secrets that lay hidden in the shadows along life's path. Many of these techniques have been practiced for centuries and can allow us to attune our own natural intuitions with the forces of the universe, enabling us to decipher signs and messages with great clarity.

Signs of the Zodiac

Since the dawn of time, mankind has looked to the heavens for guidance and answers to the mysteries of life. The ancient science of astrology is based upon the belief that the position of the constellations and other celestial bodies at the time of one's birth dictate specific personality traits.

The following pages list the twelve signs of the Western Zodiac, along with the unique characteristics designated by each of these astrological symbols.

FIRE   EARTH   AIR   WATER

The Signs of the Zodiac refer to the dates between which the Sun enters and leaves a particular constellation, thus the date on which one is born is referred to as their Sun sign or Zodiac sign. People born within the first few days designated to their sign are considered to be born on the cusp. Though they are governed by their ruling astrological sign, they are also influenced by the previous sign. Each planet or celestial body is said to rule one or more signs, thereby expressing its innate characteristics.

Each sign also reflects the qualities of a particular element: Fire, Earth, Air or Water, which describe temperament and compatibility in a general sense. Remember that astrology does not negate the existence of free will, nor does it mean one's fate is absolute and unalterable. It is merely used to describe tendencies in the character of an individual, to warn of the possibility of danger, to foresee an oncoming challenge or opportunity, and to advise how to react to such circumstances when they do arrive. Being aware of one's characteristics enables one to make more informed decisions in any given circumstance. Using what you know of yourself and of others provides you with a better ability to achieve a goal or to avoid future conflict.

ARIES

THE RAM / MARCH 21 TO APRIL 20 / FIRE SIGN
RULED BY MARS / IDEAL MATES: LEO, SAGITTARIUS
Those born under the sign of Aries possess great courage of spirit. Their self-confidence, initiative and direct approach to life make them successful leaders and pioneers who are capable of surmounting any difficulties that may stand in their path. The typical Aries enjoys action and exhibits high levels of energy, however they can be impatient, arrogant, and easily deceived or seduced.

TAURUS

THE BULL / APRIL 21 TO MAY 20 / EARTH SIGN
RULED BY VENUS / IDEAL MATES: VIRGO, CAPRICORN
Those born under the sign of Taurus have a great love of beauty and a deep appreciation for harmony in nature. They are highly imaginative yet practical, which is to say that their imagination is tempered with common sense. They are hard-working, focused, tenacious and honest, yet they have a tendency to be somewhat imposing at times.

GEMINI

THE TWINS / MAY 21 TO JUNE 21 / AIR SIGN

RULED BY MERCURY / IDEAL MATES: AQUARIUS, LIBRA

Those born under the sign of Gemini exhibit a duality of mind and character. They are quite versatile, tending to be both enthusiastic and subtle by nature. Geminis are intellectual, refined, sympathetic and cordial. They are also known for being inventive and tactful. They crave change and therefore they love to travel, however, they have a tendency to be fickle and somewhat unreliable.

CANCER

THE CRAB / JUNE 22 TO JULY 22 / WATER SIGN

RULED BY THE MOON / IDEAL MATES: PISCES, SCORPIO

Those born under the sign of Cancer are sensitive and have an enduring spirit. They are hard working, good with money, and devoted to family. Cancers tend to be conventional, reserved and somewhat guarded in their affairs. They are persistent and shrewd by nature and exhibit a good sense of foresight, however they have a tendency to be suspicious.

LEO

THE LION / JULY 23 TO AUG 22 / FIRE SIGN

RULED BY THE SUN / IDEAL MATES: ARIES, SAGITTARIUS

Those born under the sign of Leo possess great courage and leadership qualities. They are extremely affectionate and sympathetic to the needs of others. Leos are noble, defiant, direct and open, sometimes to the extent of being tactless. They are ambitious, fortunate with money, and have extravagant tastes, although, at times they may be boastful and ostentatious.

VIRGO

THE VIRGIN / AUG 23 TO SEPT 22 / EARTH SIGN

RULED BY MERCURY / IDEAL MATES: TAURUS, CAPRICORN

Those born under the sign of Virgo are calm, modest, level-headed, and practical. They are tactful and cunning, and can adapt easily to any situation. Virgos are typically intellectual and highly organized people, with a love for art and literature. They are precise and methodical, however, at times these traits border on obsessiveness. Though generally affectionate and caring, they can also seem aloof and cold-hearted.

LIBRA

THE SCALES / SEPT 23 TO OCT 22

AIR SIGN / RULED BY VENUS

IDEAL MATES: AQUARIUS, GEMINI

Those born under the sign of Libra are gentle and courteous, and constantly strive for harmony. They are generally broad-minded and tolerant, and make affectionate and loyal friends. Libras are intuitive and inventive, and though fond of change and travel, they are also natural homemakers. The pliant nature of Libra makes them somewhat complacent and gullible at times.

SCORPIO

THE SCORPION / OCT 23 TO NOV 21

WATER SIGN / RULED BY MARS

IDEAL MATES: PISCES, CANCER

Those born under the sign of Scorpio have a magnetic and complex personality. Lovers of intrigue, they are subtle, cool and secretive in their ways. They are intense in their emotions and often exhibit pronounced psychic abilities. Ambitious and idealistic, Scorpios are quite tenacious, and occasionally stubborn in their ways. They are sometimes vain and have been known to take advantage of others.

SAGITTARIUS

THE ARCHER / NOV 22 TO DEC 21

FIRE SIGN / RULED BY JUPITER

IDEAL MATES: ARIES, LEO

Those born under the sign of Sagittarius are frank, sincere, and optimistic, with a strong sense of justice. They are sociable yet fiercely independent. Sagittarians are versatile and impulsive in their actions. Humane and generous, they are also intuitive and fond of offering advice. Sagittarians are athletic and strong-willed, making them intense, hard workers. They are deep thinkers, who can, however, be judgmental, patronizing and harsh at times.

CAPRICORN

THE GOAT / DEC 22 TO JAN 19
EARTH SIGN / RULED BY SATURN
IDEAL MATES: TAURUS, VIRGO

Those born under the sign of Capricorn are methodical, diligent and critical. Though they make true friends, they also make bitter enemies and can be quite vindictive. They are generally secretive and at times, brooding, often keeping their true feelings to themselves. Capricorns exhibit great patience and caution, and have a tendency to harbor jealous feelings.

AQUARIUS

THE WATER-BEARER / JAN 20 TO FEB 18
AIR SIGN / RULED BY SATURN AND URANUS
IDEAL MATES: GEMINI, LIBRA

Those born under the sign of Aquarius are idealistic, generous and humane. They are intuitive and logical, making them good judges of human nature. Aquarians are generally cautious by nature, and though somewhat timid and opinionated, they make cheerful and reliable friends. They embody the characteristics of the classic romantic, holding truth and beauty in the highest esteem.

PISCES

THE FISH / FEB 19 TO MAR 20
WATER SIGN / RULED BY JUPITER AND NEPTUNE
IDEAL MATES: CANCER, SCORPIO

Those born under the sign of Pisces are visionaries, gifted with rich imagination. They are kind-hearted, emotional, romantic and self-sacrificing. Pisces are orderly and somewhat conventional, however, they are also superstitious and have a genuine interest in the mysteries of the unknown. They are lovers of music, arts and literature, and are often talented in these fields, though they sometimes suffer from feelings of self-doubt.

THE MYSTIC RUNES

Talismans from a forgotten
age, The Mystic Runes
have been used by those
seeking to foretell the future
and divine life's path.
Runic letters etched in
stones may either be cast
or arranged in a circle to
reveal one's fate.

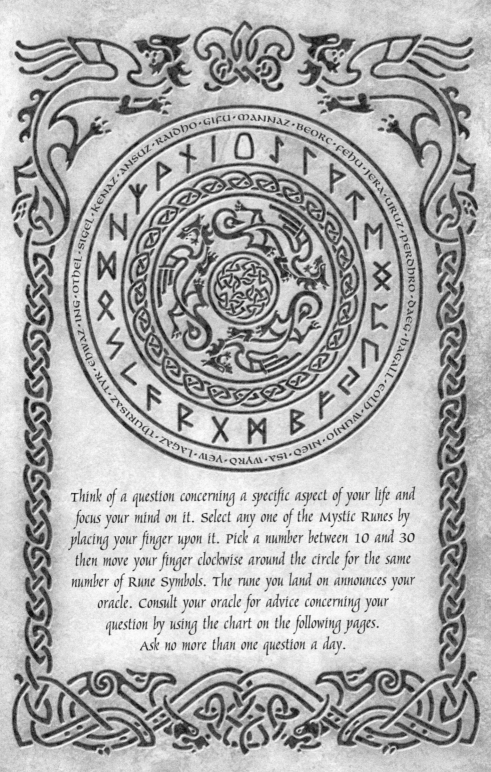

Think of a question concerning a specific aspect of your life and focus your mind on it. Select any one of the Mystic Runes by placing your finger upon it. Pick a number between 10 and 30 then move your finger clockwise around the circle for the same number of Rune Symbols. The rune you land on announces your oracle. Consult your oracle for advice concerning your question by using the chart on the following pages.

Ask no more than one question a day.

ORACLE OF THE RUNES

WYRD
THE UNKNOWABLE: This mysterious oracle, traditionally represented by a blank stone, foretells no prophecy other than to trust in destiny and allow fate to take its course.

YEW
PERSEVERANCE: This sign indicates that the goal you wish to attain is within reach. Try to view obstacles from a different perspective.

LAGAZ
FLOW: This principal rune is one of intuitive knowledge, imagination and artistic creativity. Your are being guided and protected by higher powers. Trust in prophetic dreams.

THURISAZ
WINDFALL: This rune foretells of good luck and protection. Good fortune will come unexpectedly. Recognize this lucky streak for what it truly is.

TYR

WARRIOR: This rune symbolizes extreme motivation and confidence. You will have a winning, competitive spirit in matters of business and romance. Believe in yourself.

EHWAZ

MOVEMENT: This rune foretells of a steady progress. Your horizons are broadening. Be prepared to adapt.

ING

FERTILITY: This rune concerns the family. It predicts a genesis in your home life, a new birth, a marriage, or the beginning of a healing process.

PERDHRO

INITIATION: This sign represents things shrouded in mystery. It stresses the importance of following your intuition. This rune also signifies occult abilities and second chances.

URUZ

STRENGTH: This is a sign of determination and vitality. A beneficial change will bring about new responsibilities.

JERA

HARVEST: This rune symbolizes the reaping of rewards for that which you have sown. Your hard work, patience' and perseverance will soon pay off.

FEHU

POSSESSIONS: This is a positive omen of fulfillment and material gain. This symbolizes the reward for overcoming obstacles in your path.

BEORC

GROWTH: This is the symbol of achievement regarding the ultimate completion of an idea or dream. It also signifies fertility, birth, family and renewal.

MANNAZ

THE SELF: This sign embodies your positive character traits. You have the power within yourself to conquer any adversity.

GIFU

PARTNERSHIP: This rune signifies a meeting of minds and hearts. A collective effort will be rewarding. In love, this denotes a solid relationship.

RAIDHO

JOURNEY: This rune indicates travel or the arrival of good news. Keep an open mind and be prepared to change your current course.

ANSUZ

SAGE: This rune indicates the acquisition of knowledge. You will be tested and may require advice from someone who possesses more experience or wisdom.

KENAZ

OPENING: This optimistic symbol represents a beginning or renewal in affairs of the heart. This is also a good omen that foretells of a healing or cure.

SIGEL

WHOLENESS: This positive omen is one of great power. You will be very successful in your endeavors, and any opposition encountered may be swiftly overcome.

OTHEL

BEQUEST: This rune is linked to legacies of material goods or heritage. Be frugal and patient.

DAEG

BREAKTHROUGH: This rune signifies prosperity and personal improvement. It represents the light after darkness, and triumph over adversity.

HAGALL

DISRUPTION: This rune represents forces beyond your control. Expect delays due to random events and avoid any unnecessary risks at this time.

EOLH

PROTECTION: A very positive omen foretelling of a fortunate new influence, either physical or spiritual. Trust in your instincts and you will be protected from misfortune.

WUNJO

JOY: This rune foretells of physical and emotional pleasure derived from selfless deeds. It indicates a positive outcome of any present dilemma.

NIED

CONSTRAINT: This rune symbolizes patience and discipline. Take the time to plan carefully before leaping into action. Don't act on impulse.

ISA

STANDSTILL: This involves obstacles in your relations. You may experience passivity, a loss of motivation or a decline in passion.

Divination by Dreams

Each night as we sleep we enter a fantastic realm with boundaries as limitless as our own imagination. The domain of dreams is inhabited by surreal visions of beauty as well as terrifying nightmares. Some dreams are forgotten soon after we awaken, while others leave us with vivid lasting impressions.

Experts agree that dreams are a window to the subconscious mind, and many believe that, if interpreted correctly, they are a revelation of future events as well.

Leave the waking
world behind
And take to flight
on raven's wings—
Explore the boundaries
of your mind,
And share the night
with queens and kings.
Discover secrets
buried deep,
And dare to dream
at any cost—
Cross the threshold
as you sleep,
For without dreams,
all hope is lost.

The Oracle of Dreams

For centuries, deciphering dreams has been used as way of divining the future. Modern psychoanalysts concur that specific characters and actions encountered in a person's dream represent manifestations of the subconscious mind and may be interpreted as different things, depending upon their significance to each individual. However, visionaries believe that certain dreams contain vivid premonitions of events that have yet to unfold. The following list contains many of the most common dreams and their interpretations.

People

To meet the person you love in a dream is a positive and hopeful sign that the time is right to act upon your feelings. If you talk with a king in your dreams it means that your plans are not practical, however if you are embraced or kissed by a king, you will receive the good favor and support of a powerful person. To dream that you are eating with an enemy is a sign of reconciliation.

Personal Appearance

To dream of being naked is a sign that your secrets will be exposed. To dream of your hair looking well groomed and neat foretells success and good fortune. To see yourself with white hair in a dream is a positive sign that you will succeed in your endeavors. To dream that you are cutting your hair denotes a loss of sexual empowerment. If you dream that your hair is falling out, it is an omen of great danger. To dream that your teeth are falling out denotes an illness or loss of prestige, however if you dream that you lose a tooth and it grows again it means that you will benefit from an unexpected piece of good fortune.

Actions

To dream that you are flying means that you will achieve great things. Climbing a mountain denotes strength and good luck. To dream of falling from a great height represents a fear of losing control in your personal affairs. To dream that you are running swiftly signifies strength and means that you will not be impeded in achieving your goal, but if you are running through mud, it is an omen of misfortune. To dream of walking slowly and steadily foretells you will achieve success through hard work. If you dream that you are walking straight forward along a path, it means that you will triumph over difficulties, obstacles and foes. To see yourself laughing in a dream is a sign that you will cry before the day is done. Likewise, to see yourself weeping in a dream denotes that happiness will soon be yours.

Surroundings

To dream of being engulfed and surrounded by darkness, is a sign that your enemies are plotting against you. If you dream that you are deep underground, it means that you are in danger of losing the one you love. To dream of a storm or earthquake denotes turmoil and catastrophe for those in authority. If you see a tower fall in your dream, it is an omen of death for a high-ranking official. To dream of a tree full of leaves is a sign  of realized ambition, however if you dream of a barren tree it means that your current attempts to achieve success will be in vain. If you dream that you are seated atop a stone wall or mountain, it is a positive sign that your future will be stable. If you see your house in a state of disrepair, you will suffer a loss of material wealth.

Objects

To dream of holding keys foretells of obstacles along the path to attaining your goals. A key may also represent male sexual potency. To dream of holding a book is a sign of prestige and denotes that you will go far in the world. If you see a clock in your dream, it is a sign that you will not be prepared when opportunities arise. To receive a present in your dream is an omen of imminent success. If you dream that you are wearing a necklace it means that you are in danger of losing your freedom. To see or wear pearls in your dream foretells of affliction, tears and mourning. To dream of holding an axe is a sign that you will overcome any obstacles you may encounter. To hold a sword in a dream is a warning of impending danger, however to break a sword in your dream foretells triumph over one's enemies.

Food and Drink

To dream of eating eggs denotes success and financial gain, however if you are holding eggs in your dream but do not eat them, it is a sign of sorrow and disgrace. To dream of eating something sweet is a sign of bitter disappointment. If you dream that you are eating lettuce, it is a warning of impending illness, but if you are eating meat, it is a sign that you will be rewarded for the actions of

someone else. If you eat fish in a dream, it is a sign that your plans will not succeed. To dream of olives or grapes is a positive omen for a prosperous future. To dream of drinking wine foretells struggles with obstacles in your path, but if wine is spilled in your dream, it means that your troubles will soon end. To see or drink milk in your dreams is a sign that your adversaries will fail in their plans against you.

Animals

To dream of a black horse means that your plans will fail. If you fall from a horse in your dream it means that you will suffer a physical or monetary setback. If you see a wolf yawning in your dream you should be wary of empty promises. To dream of a dog barking foretells an attack from an enemy. To see a lion warns of a conflict with a powerful adversary. Seeing a cat in your dream represents prosperity and feminine sexuality, however if the cat in your dream is black, it is an omen of bad luck. To dream of a rabbit before setting out on a voyage is an omen that you will encounter misfortune on your trip. To dream of watching fish swim denotes maturity, curiosity and self discovery.

Birds

To dream of a raven or crow means that you will receive bad news and should beware treachery and shameful action. To see an eagle or hawk flying in your dream denotes that the dream itself is a warning from God, however to capture a bird of prey in a dream is an omen of success. To dream of a white dove is a very positive omen of good fortune, friendship and love. To dream of a rooster is a sign

that you will attain your heart's desire. To hold a partridge in your dream denotes that the person you love shares the same feelings for you. To let birds escape your care in a dream is a sign of personal loss.

Snakes

To dream of walking on serpents is an omen of triumph over your enemies. To dream of snakes in your bed is a positive omen of strength and male sexual potency. To dream of being chased by snakes or reptiles is an omen to beware dangerous enemies.

Insects

To dream of wasps means danger and attacks from your enemies. To dream that you are holding a bee denotes that your hopes will meet with disappointment. If you dream of worms, it means you will be troubled by a host of annoyances. To dream of spiders denotes that your plans are well-laid. If you dream of beetles or roaches, it means that you worries will be many.

Water

To dream of a rapidly flowing river is an omen of success and triumph over obstacles and enemies. To dream of a clear fountain or washing one's hands or feet denotes that your troubles will soon come to an end. To dream of swimming in the sea or drinking muddy water is an omen of sickness. To dream of diving into a body of water denotes danger or an unpredictable dilemma. To dream of a stormy sea is an omen of turmoil in your personal affairs, whereas dreaming of a calm sea denotes success.

Fire

To dream of a fire raging out of control denotes strength, power and anger. To dream of being enveloped in smoke or fog means that you will be overcome by a stressful situation and that you should proceed with caution. To dream of being burned denotes that you may be involved in a scandal or that a personal secret will be exposed. To dream of burning coals or incense foretells that you are vulnerable to danger, however to hold a wax candle in your dream is a sign of good fortune.

Heavenly Bodies

To see stars falling is an omen of great danger. To see a clear night sky full of stars denotes a future with limitless prospects and possibilities. If you dream of a bright sun shining in the sky it means that you will gain recognition and praise for your achievements. To dream of the dawning sun signifies new prospects on the horizon, while dreaming of the setting sun means that a current phase of your life is coming to an end. To dream of a full moon denotes sexual passion and desire, whereas a partial moon signifies that your feelings may be unrequited.

The Wheel of Fortune

The Mystical Wheel of
Fortune provides a key to
understanding the mysteries
along life's path. The Wheel
has been the subject of various
works of art and literature
since ancient times.
Representing universal balance
and change, the Wheel can be
used as a method of foretelling
future events.

Consult the wheel once a day to forecast coming events.

Begin by focusing your mind on a question concerning a specific aspect of your life as you move your finger around the outer circle. Let your intuition be your guide as you select one of the twelve elemental symbols. Make note of the symbol settled upon, then choose a number between 10 and 20 and move your finger in a clockwise direction along the central lines of the Wheel. Make note of the second symbol you settle upon, then choose another number between 10 and 20 and move your finger in a clockwise direction along the central lines one final time. Make note of the three symbols you have randomly selected, then consult the Oracle of the Wheel on the following pages to interpret your fortune.

△△△ **Patience**—Exercise caution, and reflect upon your current situation as you wait things out.

△△▽ **Gain**—You will attain something that your heart desires.

△△△ **Desire**—Physical desires and secret passions will be fulfilled.

△△▽ **Nemesis**—Opposing forces interfere with your plans. Be prepared to face conflict.

△▽△ **Harmony**—A combined effort will produce beautiful results.

△▽▽ **Friendship**—Kindred spirits share common interests and support one another.

△▽△ **Setback**—Present circumstances force you to rethink your current plan before moving forward.

△▽▽ **Solitude**—Spend time alone to contemplate your current situation.

△△△ **Obstacle**—A barrier temporarily keeps you from attaining your goal. Try a new approach.

△△▽ **Sage Advice**—Seek the wisdom of someone with more experience. Ask questions.

△△△ **Action**—Be motivated. This is not a time to stand still or be idle. Action is required.

△△▽ **Soulmates**—You are destined to know true love. Your spiritual soulmate is near.

△▽△ **Stagnation**—You have reached a point of impasse and cannot grow without making changes.

△▽▽ **Partnership**—Two separate forces join together to achieve a unified goal.

△▽△ **Adventure**—Be daring and spontaneous. Take a bold risk and see where it leads you.

△▽▽ **Secrets**—True emotions lie hidden. Someone admires you from afar.

▽ △ △ **Wisdom**—Think before you act. Use your knowledge and experience to make a wise choice.

▽ △ ▽ **Health**—Your physical strengths will allow you to achieve your desired goals.

▽ △ △ **Distress**—You will experience a temporary period of sorrow. It's always darkest before the dawn.

▽ △ ▽ **Rejuvenation**—An invigorating energy will replenish your strength.

▽ ▽ △ **Loss**—You will suffer the loss of something very dear to you. Cherish what you still have.

▽ ▽ ▽ **Boredom**—Habitual patterns may result in a loss of interest. Try something new.

▽ ▽ △ **Steady Progress**—Perseverance on your current path will garner positive results in the long run.

▽ ▽ ▽ **Success**—Your current course of action will allow you to achieve your desired goal

▽ △ △ **Pain**—Your current situation will cause emotional distress and may lead to physical pain.

▽ △ ▽ **Exploration**—Trying new things leads to enlightening experiences. Entertain new possibilities.

▽ △ △ **Wealth**—You will receive a payment which could amount to a considerable sum of money.

▽ △ ▽ **Love**—You will share a deep emotional and physical bond with your partner. Romance blossoms.

▽ ▽ △ **Meditation**—A quiet time of inner reflection allows you to relax and see things clearer.

▽ ▽ ▽ **Magic**—Mystical forces surround you and help you attain your goal. Believe in your dreams.

▽ ▽ △ **Art**—Be creative and follow your artistic muse. Express yourself through imagery.

▽ ▽ ▽ **Punishment**—A guilty party will pay for their past offenses.

WRITING— Keep a journal of your thoughts and creative musings. Develop your ideas.

CATASTROPHE—Beware a drastic turn of events and brace to weather a coming storm.

LUCK—Good fortune will shine upon you. Be careful not to push your luck.

SERENDIPITY—A strange coincidence will lead to a fortunate reward.

FORGIVENESS—Now is the time to relinquish past grudges and forgive indiscretions.

CREATIVITY—Nurture your imagination and develop your original ideas.

LUST—A strong sexual attraction leads to fulfilled passions without emotional commitment.

ALLIANCE—Teamwork will allow you to succeed in reaching a common goal.

HEALING—Physical and emotional growth has made you stronger. Old wounds cease to hurt.

HASTE—Swift action is required. Be prepared to think fast and move quickly.

SACRIFICE—You will have to relinquish something you cherish in order to attain your goal.

DEATH—A current situation comes to an drastic end. An ending leads to a new beginning.

HARDSHIP—Be prepared to struggle and experience difficulty on your current path.

REWARD—You will receive recognition and reap the benefits of your labors.

MUSIC—Fill your life with songs that inspire you. Strive for harmony in all you do.

INTUITION—Let your inner voice be your guide to great things. Follow your heart.

▽△△ **Family**—Spending time with family has its own rewards. Make the most of your time together.

▽△▽ **Journey**—A voyage will bring great pleasure. Visit somewhere you are curious about.

▽△△ **Animals**—The affection of an animal lends emotional support.

▽△▽ **Gifts**—You will receive a thoughtful gift. Be thankful and use it wisely.

▽▽△ **Turmoil**—An unexpected turn of events could cause confusion. Don't get distracted.

▽▽▽ **Celebration**—Enjoy a festive time to celebrate a recent achievement.

▽▽△ **Opposites Attract**—Two hearts with different interests share a curious bond.

▽▽▽ **Performance**—Concentrate and stay focused in your daily routine. Practice makes perfect.

▽△△ **Heartbreak**—Passionate feelings are not returned. Redirect your romantic pursuits.

▽△▽ **Misunderstanding**—Confusion arises from a simple miscommunication. Talk things over.

▽△△ **Apology**—A sorry soul will make amends for an error in judgment.

▽△▽ **Fate**—Universal forces intervene in your affairs. Trust in fate.

▽▽△ **Reason**—Use logic and deduction to solve a current problem. Don't let emotions blind you.

▽▽▽ **Reunion**—You will soon be reunited with someone from your past.

▽▽△ **Wild Revelry**—Shed your inhibitions to celebrate a joyous time. Live for today.

▽▽▽ **Respect**—Be considerate of others and honor those who are deserving.

The Art of Palm Reading

Palmistry is the study of the major mounts and lines of the hand to interpret one's fate. These markings differ greatly, making each person unique. The left hand represents inherent character qualities. The right hand signifies how well a person develops such traits and is a map that can be deciphered to reveal your life's path. Differences between both hands indicate change. The more differences the more changes have been made or imposed. The more similar the two hands, the more the person is content and less likely to alter their lifestyle. Consult the descriptions on the following pages to interpret what the particular markings on your own palm represent.

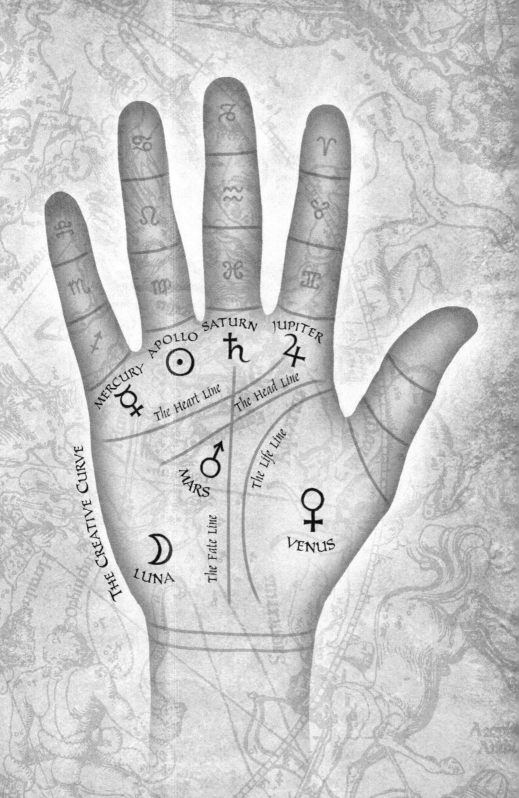

MERCURY
APOLLO SATURN JUPITER

THE CREATIVE CURVE

The Heart Line
The Head Line
The Life Line

MARS

LUNA

The Fate Line

VENUS

The Mounts

The fleshy, padded areas of the palm and at the base of each finger are called mounts. Each mount is associated with certain social, mental, or emotional aspects. A round mount is somewhat raised and smoothly rounded, and considered ideal. A peaked mount is very obviously raised and may appear slightly pointed, while a flat mount is really not plainly distinguishable and is about even with the rest of the palm area. Each type of mount represents different character qualities regarding the aspects of the given mount.

The Jupiter Mount

Represents pride, integrity, ambition and spirituality.
ROUND: good social sense, charm, leadership qualities
PEAKED: selfish, overbearing nature, arrogance, bigotry
FLAT: laziness, strong dislike for authority, low ambition

The Saturn Mount

Represents strength of character and mental stability.
ROUND: plain, commonsense approach to life
PEAKED: gloomy, cynical, unforgiving, overly sensitive
FLAT: lacking a sense of humor, given to irresponsibility.

The Apollo Mount

Represents creativity, artistic appreciation and sociability.
ROUND: bright, cheerful disposition, inventive
PEAKED: sentimental, over alert, ostentatious, narcissistic
FLAT: lack of refinement, dull personality

The Mercury Mount

Represents communication abilities.
ROUND: witty, commercially talented
PEAKED: prone to taking chances, possibly self-deceptive
FLAT: poor ability for self-expression

The Venus Mount

Represents physical energy and level of libido.
ROUND: excellent stamina and vitality
PEAKED: more than healthy sex drive, zest for life
FLAT: cold natured, prone to selfishness and family strife

☽ The Luna Mount

Represents imagination, subconscious and intuitive powers.
ROUND: artistically creative
PEAKED: caring, peaceful and harmonious
FLAT: hesitant, non-imaginative

♂ The Plain of Mars

Located in the center of the palm and to be studied by touch. This area reflects how one interacts with their immediate environment. If area feels fleshy or spongy there is an interest in worldly affairs. If area is thin and bony this person has little interest in the happenings around them.

The Creative Curve

This is the outer curved edge of the palm. The more obvious this curve the greater one's creative energy. If the curve is more pronounced at the top one might have more mental creativity, but lack the ability to carry out ideas. If curved in the middle, the person is skilled at bringing concepts to life, while a curve at the bottom indicates a more practical personality.

THE LINES

Lines may appear heavily etched or faint, wide or thin, uninterrupted, broken, or frayed. Lines may be closer or farther from other lines, they may cross other major lines, and hence be influenced by the aspects of the crossing line. Lines may start nearer to the edge of the palm or more inside the palm. The clearer and more defined the line, the stronger its meaning. The more fragmented a line is, the more disruption a person can expect in regards to what the particular line signifies, the weaker it is.

THE HEAD LINE

Represents intelligence, perceptiveness, reasoning and world view.

LENGTH: The shorter the line the more practical a person is. A longer line indicates more imaginative thinking, a more flexible attitude. A head line that extends all the way across the palm indicates excellent mental control.

POSITION: The higher the line starts on the Jupiter mount the more honorable the person. The wider the gap between head and heart lines, the more "down to earth" the person is. The narrower this gap, the more emotional and indecisive the person. The wider the gap between the start of the head and life

Effort Lines

lines, the more impulsive the person is likely to be. A head line that starts within the life line signifies a follower. If the end of the line sweeps down toward the Luna mount this represents an over active imagination, a person prone to flights of fancy.

Broken Line: Expect a change of lifestyle.

Chains

Forked Line: A fork at the end signifies an investigative mind. A short fork with one line pointing up is called "the writer's hook" and indicates the likelihood this person will be recognized for their creative talent, possibly gaining fame.

Chained Line: Suggests a lack of concentration.

Trident

Wide or Shallow Line: This person is easily discouraged.

Deeply Etched Line: If deeper and more defined than the life line, the head rules, physical activities come secondary. This person may also be egotistical and loves flattery.

Frayed Line

Fine or Thin Line: A warning that physical activity must be balanced with good rest. This person tires quickly.

Faded Line: If a strong section is followed by a weak section it indicates poor self-discipline and an inability to cope with crisis.

The Heart Line

Represents emotions and how they effect your personality.

Length: Ideally this line sweeps from the Jupiter mount, curves smoothly under the other mounts, and ends at the edge of the hand below the Mercury mount. An uninterrupted, long line designates a true romantic.

Position: A high set line suggests one who intellectualizes and analyzes their emotions. A lower set path indicates a more passionate nature. If both heart and head lines are set low expect a jealous, possessive lover. If all three lines, heart, head and life, start at the same source this person can expect a serious trauma in life, emotionally, physically, or mentally.

Left vs. Right: If the left hand has a curved heart line and the right shows a straight line, then the person was most likely hurt in an earlier relationship. The opposite indicates a sympathetic soul. If each hand appears similar then all is well in love, no change is foreseen.

Broken Line: Indicates a restless nature, a constant need for change. This person will have a wide variety of acquaintances, but few really close friends. He or she will make frequent journeys.

Straight vs. Curved: The straighter the line the more materialistic the person. This lover may be more inhibited and uncomfortable with public displays of affection. A more curved line indicates a more imaginative lover, warmer and open to suggestion.

The Lucky Trident: A three-pronged branch at the source promises luck in love. However, if the lowest branch connects with the head line the emotional future looks negative, long meaningful relationships may be difficult to attain.

The Life Line

Represents well-being, vitality, energy and endurance.

Length: The actual length has no bearing on a person's duration of life, it merely indicates the quality of life and what they get out of it, or what obstacles may have to be overcome.

Position: A line that starts on the mount of Jupiter indicates a born leader. If it starts connected to the head line, there were restrictions early in life for as long as the lines continue together. If the line sweeps suddenly out it indicates an effort to attain personal freedom and self-expression.

Effort Lines: Small vertical lines that extend out and up from the life line. These are positive and represent the effort to better one's personal circumstances. If they point towards Saturn this person is a hard worker. If there is a long line branching out toward Apollo this person has enjoyed easy and early success.

Chained Line: If the line starts as a series of small islands it suggests an illegitimate, difficult or unusual birth. It indicates a possible childhood ailment and a dependence upon others. Chains appearing later on the life line indicate a weakness, or recurring illness.

Dots on the Line: Signify worries.

Bars across the Line: Indicate minor setbacks.

Frayed Line: Appearing at the end represents a weakening of the body or old age.

Broken Line: This should be viewed as serious. Beware if taking on anything hazardous during the time indicated on your timeline (see chart). Midpoint breaks correspond to midlife. When the line starts to strengthen after being previously weak, this signifies an effort to get back into the swing of things.

Second Life Line: In some cases there may be a sister line, closely following along the outside of the life line (palm side). It is usually on the left hand or on both, but rarely appears on just the right hand. If this second line is present, this person leads a double life.

The Line of Mars: If a sister line appears inside the life line (thumb side) this gives strength to whatever the life line indicates, also called an 'influence' line. If an influence line extends from Venus and crosses the life line there will be obstruction from family. If it does not touch the life line this indicates family support.

THE FATE LINE

Represents goals, ambitions and personal satisfaction.

Length & Position: Some fate lines run all the way up from the wrist to Saturn while others are much shorter. The fate line always runs vertically up the center of the palm. If a person has a straight, uninterrupted fate line that runs the entire path from wrist to Saturn, it is rare. Such a person will overcome all opposition, most likely finding a career in the public eye.

Source: Some lines start at the wrist, while others begin higher up inside the palm. The higher up a fate line starts, the later in life the person began to set their goals. If the fate line begins at the life line this indicates a need for family support for that time (see chart). Once it moves away, support is no longer needed or available. If the fate line begins inside the life line this indicates a duty or family responsibility to meet, perhaps pressure to follow a certain career path. Once it leaves the area, the person is free to do as they choose. A branched source shows conflicting interests.

Left vs. Right: If there is a fate line on the left hand only, this person is a dreamer, but not necessarily a successful one. If it appears only on the right, this person is appreciative of what they have, but seeking to improve their lot in life. Those with clear lines on both hands are well-balanced, responsible, aware, and do well socially. If the fate line is absent altogether, this indicates little ambition and poor social skills.

Forked Fate Line: Any fork in the fate line suggests fame, fortune or both. Note where the 2 branches point:

> JUPITER & APOLLO—a high-profile career such as politics.
> SATURN & MERCURY—medical research or commercial enterprise.
> JUPITER & MERCURY—banking, stock market, or other financial career.
> SATURN & APOLLO—theatrical performer.

Influences: When the fate merges with the heart line, an emotional decision may negatively influence career goals. A fork directly on the heart line means this person has good instincts, will weigh their options and arrive at the correct decision. When a fork appears between the heart and head lines, look at which is closer. If closer to the heart, then changes will be based on instinct. If closer to the head, changes will be made for practical reasons.

The Line of Milieu: A line appearing between the life and fate lines indicates a late bloomer and suggests problems getting started. These could be financial, family or health problems, or some other obstacle to overcome.

The Marriage Line: If fate merges with a line coming from the Luna mount, this indicates a happy marriage or a close and dependable friendship.

MEASURING AGE ALONG THE LINES

The Life Line can be divided in half, which is roughly equivalent to age 35, then keep dividing the remaining halves to get other ages. This also works for the heart and head lines. Remember that the life line, heart, and head lines all begin on the thumb side of the hand.

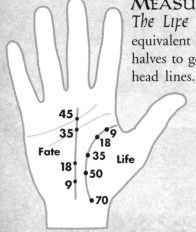

The Fate Line starts at the wrist and is measured bottom to top. Where it crosses the heart and head lines, the corresponding ages are 45 and 35. Midway down from 35 to the source of the fate line is about equal to age 18–20. Keep dividing in half to get other ages.

Secrets of the I Ching

The I Ching or "Book of Changes" was developed 4,000 years ago by Chinese shamans as an oracle that served as a guide to the path of enlightenment. During the 4th century BC, the sage and philosopher Confucius popularized the use of the I Ching for meditation and spiritual growth. Since then, the I Ching has been used as a method of divination for learning from the past and seeking guidance along future paths.

THE 8 TRIGRAMS OF THE PA KUA

The traditional arrangement of the eight Trigrams is called a PA KUA. It is often combined with the TAI CHI in the center, a symbol representing the opposing forces of the Universe: the YIN, or negative forces, and the YANG, the positive forces. The Later Heaven Arrangement (shown above) is attributed to first emperor Wen of the Chou dynasty, who expanded the I Ching to include the 64 hexagrams. The FANG-SHENG (shown on the following page) includes an 8-sided star or octagram, and represents the Early Heaven Arrangement of the Pa Kua, and is often used in magic rituals as a charm to protect against harmful influences.

THE PRIMARY ELEMENTS (GUA) OF THE I-CHING

Ch'ien (Heaven) Creative, limitless potential and vitality.
Associations—body part: head, color: white, animal: horse

Chen (Thunder) Exciting, spontaneous, powerful and relentless.
Associations—body part: foot, color: red, animal: dragon

K'an (Water) Mysterious and deep, dangerous and fearless.
Associations—body part: ear, color: blue, animal: pig

Ken (Mountain) Still, calm and meditative.
Associations—body part: hand, color: purple, animal: dog

K'un (Earth) Receptive, nurturing, devoted.
Associations—body part: abdomen, color: black, animal: cow

Sun (Wind) Gentle and penetrating, flexible and strong.
Associations—body part: thighs, color: green, animal: tiger

Li (Fire) Consuming yet productive, beautiful and intelligent.
Associations—body part: eyes, color: orange, animal: peacock

Tui (Lake) Joyful, sensual and attractive.
Associations—body part: mouth and lips, color: yellow, animal: sheep

FINDING YOUR DAILY HEXAGRAM

Each consultation of the I Ching is accomplished by a random selection of a pair of trigrams, placing one on top of the other to form a hexagram. Traditionally, this method of divination employed a set of yarrow sticks, with some being knotted or painted with "breaks" while others remained smooth or solid. The modern method uses coins to attain the 64 hexagrams.

1.) Select 3 coins with "heads" and "tails" markings. Assign to each side these values: heads=3, tails=2. Keep paper and pencil handy. Now, hold the coins while meditating a few moments on your question.

2.) You will toss your coins a total of 6 times. Each time you do, add together the values of the heads and tails that appear, then determine if the final result is an odd or even number. For example, you might throw two heads(6) and one tail(2) = 8 (even) -or- one head(3) and two tails(4) = 7 (odd).

3.) Draw a yin line (– –) for each even-numbered result. Draw a yang line (—) for each odd-numbered result. Begin drawing from the bottom, and build upward. You should end up with six lines, forming two sets of trigrams stacked one upon the other. This is your hexagram.

For example, it might look like...

6th toss = even	– –	
5th toss = odd	—	} Upper Trigram
4th toss = even	– –	
3th toss = even	– –	
2nd toss = even	– –	} Lower Trigram
1st toss = odd	—	

4.) Consult the keymap to find the number of your hexagram. Find your upper trigram among the top horizontal row, locate your lower trigram along the vertical column, then find your hexagram number where the row and column intersect. Look up the number on the following pages to discover your fortune.

HEXAGRAM KEYMAP

UPPER → / LOWER ↓	CH'IEN Heaven	CH'EN Thunder	K'AN Water	KÊN Mountain	K'UN Earth	SUN Wind	LI Fire	TUI Lake
CH'IEN Heaven	1	34	5	26	11	9	14	43
CH'EN Thunder	25	51	3	27	24	42	21	17
K'AN Water	6	40	29	4	7	59	64	47
KÊN Mountain	33	62	39	52	15	53	56	31
K'UN Earth	12	16	8	23	2	20	35	45
SUN Wind	44	32	48	18	46	57	50	28
LI Fire	13	55	63	22	36	37	30	49
TUI Lake	10	54	60	41	19	61	38	58

THE 64 HEXAGRAMS DEFINED

乾 ䷀ 1. Ch'ien (The Creative) Follow your creative instincts and you will meet with good fortune.

坤 ䷁ 2. K'un (The Receptive) Be accepting and yielding to nourish your creative energies. Keep an open mind.

屯 ䷂ 3. Chun (Difficult Beginnings) The current situation requires strength, perseverance, and the will to try again.

蒙 ䷃ 4. Mêng (Youthful Folly) The experience of elder wisdom will help you to attain your heart's desire.

需 ䷄ 5. Hsu (Waiting) Patience is required at this time. Remain calm and wait for a better time to act.

訟 ䷅ 6. Sung (Conflict) Avoid conflict by stepping back. Retain your integrity and do not allow yourself to enter the fray.

師 ䷆ 7. Shih (The Army) Action against opposition should be tempered with restraint and compassion.

比 ䷇ 8. Pi (Union) Strive for a harmonious union between two forces that compliment and assist one another.

小畜 ䷈ 9. Hsiao Ch'u (Small Steps) Don't be hasty or forceful. You will gradually attain your goal by way of firm footholds and small steps.

履 ䷉ 10. Lu (Conduct) Remain steadfast and light of heart but tread carefully through a dangerous situation.

泰 ䷊ 11. T'ai (Peace) Harmony and bliss can be maintained by a peaceful heart and mind. Seek a healthy balance of body and spirit.

否 ䷋ 12. P'i (Standstill) Your current goals are blocked but not thwarted. Take some time to reflect upon your situation and form a new strategy.

13. T'ung Jên (Fellowship with Others) Cooperation between peers will allow you to attain a mutual goal. Work together as equals.

14. Ta Yu (Abundant Possession) Clear thinking and humble actions will lead to great reward. You are on the right path.

15. Ch'ien (Modesty) Be humble and respectful. Do not seek recognition for your actions but be content with the result.

16. Yu (Enthusiasm) An energetic and cheerful attitude will enable you to attain your present goal.

17. Sui (Following) Observe the truth and act accordingly. Sage advice will guide you.

18. Ku (Repair Damage) That which has been ruined by neglect can be redeemed through effort. Work to mend corruption and decay.

19. Lin (Approach) Good things are coming your way. The path you are following leads to success.

20. Kuan (Contemplation) Meditate on your current situation for the answer you seek. You can influence others by setting an example.

21. Shih Ho (Biting Through) Clear thinking and decisive action will allow you to overcome an aggressive obstacle. Stubbornness will only make matters worse.

22. Bei (Grace) True beauty comes from within. Focus on spiritual attributes rather than the physical or material aspects.

23. Po (Splitting Apart) Weather the current storm and proceed when it has passed. You will not prevail with any action at this time.

24. Fu (Return) You have reached a turning point. Your horizons are bright and your situation will improve.

25. Wu Wang (Innocence) Trust the intuition and innocence of your inner spirit. Remain pure and sincere.

26. Ta Ch'u (Taming by the Great) Be patient and use the time to determine the best way to channel your strength and knowledge.

27. I (Nourishment) Feed your mind as you would feed your body. Positive actions and a healthy attitude nourish the spirit.

28. Ta Kuo (Preponderance of the Great) Stand firm under pressure and resist the temptation to give in. Rely on your inner strength and integrity. Bend but don't break.

29. K'an (The Abysmal) Don't despair. Stay calm and flow through troubled waters to reach a place of refuge.

30. Li (The Clinging) Hold fast to positive values which nourish your spirit. Don't abandon your principles during times of stress.

31. Hsien (Influence) Be open-minded to the ideas of others and set a good example for those who look to you for guidance. Use your wisdom to sway others.

32. Heng (Duration) Now is the time that your endurance will be tested. Be persistent and don't change your present course of action.

33. Tun (Retreat) This is a time to withdraw from the fray and conserve your energy. Retreat to a safe position and stay out of harm's way.

34. Ta Chuang (Power of the Great) By remaining patient, humble, gentle and honest you can channel the creative forces of the Universe to achieve great things.

35. Chin (Progress) You are making progress and moving forward. Distance yourself from bad influences to advance to your full potential.

36. 明夷 ䷣ **Ming I (Darkening of the Light)** When times are darkest, don't succumb to despair, but instead rely on your inner light to guide you.

37. 家人 ䷤ **Chia Jen (The Family)** You need the strength of a good foundation, firm structure and a wise leader for your plan to succeed. Work together in harmony.

38. 睽 ䷥ **K'uei (Opposition)** Overcome opposition by seeking inner truth. Avoid misunderstandings based solely on outward appearances.

39. 蹇 ䷦ **Chien (Obstruction)** Re-examine your thinking through inner reflection and seek sage advice to conquer the obstacles that thwart you from your goal.

40. 解 ䷧ **Hsieh (Deliverance)** You must learn from past mistakes and relinquish old habits in order to reach your goal.

41. 損 ䷨ **Sun (Decrease)** Exercise discipline and tone things down. Your current situation requires a simple solution. Remain honest and sincere.

42. 益 ䷩ **I (Increase)** Now is a time of great progress, personal improvement and material gain. Offer help to those in need.

43. 夬 ䷪ **Kuai (Breakthrough)** Be cautious but remain resolute, and you will overcome the current obstacles in your path.

44. 姤 ䷫ **Kou (Coming To Meet)** Don't judge others based on stereotypes or past prejudices. Follow your intuition and things will proceed smoothly.

45. 萃 ䷬ **Ts'ui (Gathering Together)** Unite with others who share a common goal and work together to achieve peace and prosperity. Take the lead and remain devoted to your cause.

46. 升 ䷭ **Sheng (Pushing Upward)** Be persistent and you will make progress slowly but steadily. Savor life's journey to experience inner growth.

困䷮ **47. K'un (Oppression)** Calm inner reflection will give you the strength and wisdom that will enable you to prevail in a time of extreme adversity.

井䷯ **48. Ching (The Well)** Seek a reliable source of spiritual nourishment and tap into it, then apply your newfound strength and wisdom to aid others.

革䷰ **49. Ko (Revolution)** Be wary of your surroundings. You must undergo change in order to adapt to your new situation.

鼎䷱ **50. Ting (The Cauldron)** Act carefully and in moderation. Contributing to the greater good will earn you the recognition you deserve over time.

震䷲ **51. Chen (The Arousing)** A sleeping dragon has been awakened within you. Focus on this newfound source of inspiration and create something positive.

艮䷳ **52. Ken (Keeping Still)** Don't budge from your current position. Remain unaffected by the things that surround you. Stay calm and keep a clear mind.

漸䷴ **53. Chien (Development)** You are developing new skills that will be quite useful. When you apply your new abilities, you will serve as an inspiration for others.

歸妹䷵ **54. Kuei Mei (Marrying Maiden)** Don't act on impulse or succumb to strong emotional desires. Follow your head, not your heart at this time.

豐䷶ **55. Feng (Abundance)** Live for the moment and take full advantage of your present good fortune. Be confident but don't be arrogant.

旅䷷ **56. Lu (The Wanderer)** Be respectful of the customs and hospitality of others and don't take your current situation for granted. Let your restless spirit guide you.

巽 ䷸ **57. Xuan (The Gentle)** Use gentle persuasion and remain persistent to create long-lasting results. Don't dwell on negative influences.

兌 ䷹ **58. Tui (The Joyous)** Be more accepting and you will find harmony with others. Rely on your inner strength to become more independent. Be strong inside but let your actions be gentle.

渙 ䷺ **59. Huan (Dispersion)** A calm and soothing behavior will gradually garner positive results. Use tact and peaceful persuasion to wear down a rigid obstacle in your path.

節 ䷻ **60. Chieh (Limitation)** Understanding your own limitations allows you to choose your path wisely and achieve your goals without setbacks. Be prudent and don't attempt to live beyond your means.

中孚 ䷼ **61. Chung Fu (Inner Truth)** Cast off all prejudices to discover the universal truth of your current situation. Don't be distracted by emotions or preconceived opinions.

小過 ䷽ **62. Hsiao Kuo (Preponderance of the Small)** Free your mind of all negative influences and thoughts. Your morals are being tested. Don't succumb to pettiness, and resist the temptation to act on impulse.

既濟 ䷾ **63. Chi Chi (After Completion)** Don't dwell too long on former accomplishments. Move forward and reapply the same successful principles to attain even higher goals.

未濟 ䷿ **64. Wei Chi (Before Completion)** Your goal is within reach. Remain calm and confident under pressure, but don't become arrogant or tempestuous. A rash decision at this time could lead to downfall.

ANGELS AND DEMONS

In every culture throughout the world there exists a belief in angels and demons in one form or another. These spiritual entities are said to either watch over and protect us, or walk among us causing strife and discord. Such spirits may take the form of animals or chimera, some may appear as human, with wings or without. Some cultures do not necessarily attribute properties of "good" or "evil" to such beings, and traditions vary as to whether they have free will or are merely extensions of a divine consciousness. Whatever their purpose, these beings of light and darkness intrigue and inspire us.

VARGO 99

Angels

Good verses Evil

Ancient civilizations are rife with stories of celestial spirits that might be viewed as the early precursors of angels and demons. During the first century, the Persian Empire reformed their religion under the teachings of a prophet called Zoroaster. According to Zoroastrianism, the sun god, Ohrmazd, lived in the light, attended by seven *anisha spenta,* "immortal spirits." His dark counterpart, Ahriman, ruled the night. The two were constantly engaged in battle, Ahriman undoing the good work, and Ohrmazd undoing the evil—which included washing the world clean in a Great Flood. Good and evil deeds were recorded in a type of ledger book, which was to be consulted after one's death. If the good deeds outnumbered the bad, the person would ascend to the "House of Song." Otherwise, the soul would pass into the Netherworld to linger in solitude until the Apocalypse. Eventually, a savior—a man born of a virgin—would come to conquer evil forever and reunite the souls of the dead with their bodies.

These ideals proved very popular, providing much of the framework for other religions including Christianity, segregating the roles of angels and demons, and defining good and evil. By the 6th century the famous "Seven Deadly Sins" was firmly established, along with the "Seven Heavenly Virtues".

The Seven Deadly Sins	The Seven Holy Virtues
Pride	Humility
Envy	Kindness
Wrath	Patience
Sloth	Diligence
Avarice	Temperance
Gluttony	Abstinence
Lust	Chastity

The Nine Orders of Angels

First Sphere: Guardians

SERAPHIM—Angels of love, light, and fire, the "burning ones" or "fiery serpents." There are four Seraphim who serve as the caretakers of God's Throne and continuously sing hymns of praise. They also supervise the movement of the heavens. They have six wings; two covering their faces, two covering their legs, and two with which they fly.

CHERUBIM—Guardians of the stars. Cherubim have four faces: one of a man, ox, lion, and eagle. They have four conjoined wings covered with eyes, and cloven feet. Cherubim guard the way to the Tree of Life and the Throne of God.

THRONES—Angels of justice; also called "wheels" or "chariots."

Second Sphere: Governors

DOMINIONS—Govern the duties of lower angels. They hold an orb or scepter as an emblem of authority.

VIRTUES—Work miracles on earth and bestow grace and valor. Names associated with the Virtues are: Gabriel, Michael, Sariel, and Peliel.

POWERS—Bearers of conscience and the keepers of history. Concerned with intellectual and academic pursuits. Their duty is to oversee the distribution of power among mankind. Some beliefs hold that the Powers thwart the efforts of demons to overthrow the world, others claim they preside over demons, or are themselves evil.

Third Sphere: Messengers & Soldiers

PRINCIPALITIES—Protectors of religion. The Principalities are shown wearing a crown and carrying a scepter. Their duty is to carry out the orders given to them by the Dominions and bequeath blessings to the material world. They are also said to inspire the arts and sciences.

ARCHANGELS—Guardians of people and all physical things. Traditionally there are seven archangels, and though medieval manuscripts give varying names, only three are commonly agreed upon: Michael, Gabriel, and Raphael. Uriel or Anael are usually named as fourth, then depending on the source: Raguel, Zerachiel and Remiel; Samael, Sachiel and Cassiel and others.

ANGELS—A general classification of celestial spirit lowest in rank who act as messengers and are most concerned with the affairs of living things.

The Angels & their Charges

The nature of angels may vary between cultures, but one constant remains true: that angels serve as a conduit between mankind and his god(s). Many are given the role of warrior, and the concept of a "guardian angel" is a popular one. Following is a partial list of angels and their offices.

ARIEL—A healer and protector of nature. He is called the "Lion of God." He is also sometimes included as an Archangel.

AZRAEL—Known as the "Angel of Death," his role is primarily to help the dead on their journey, to give comfort and ensure they do not suffer.

CASSIEL (CAßIEL)—He is called the "Angel of Solitude and Tears." His role is to Watch and preside over the death of kings.

GABRIEL—Chief of the divine messengers, he is said to have heard and answered the cries of man under the crush of the Nephilim. He and the other Archangels were sent to incite a war among the giants.

GRIGORI—The name given for the 200 Fallen Angels who were cast out of Heaven. Also called "The Watchers." They were said to have sired the Nephilim.

METATRON—The "Heavenly Scribe," is said to have been the human prophet Enoch. Both he and his twin brother Sandalphon are the only angels that were once human. Metatron records the duties of the other angels. He led the Israelites to safety after their exodus from Egypt.

MICHAEL—His name means "who is alike unto God." He is usually depicted as a great warrior in full battle armor and brandishing a sword or spear, with which he pierces the infernal dragon. He is a patron angel of chivalry and the armed forces. He is likewise a healer of those wounded in battle. He led the battle against the Grigori. He is honored on Michaelmas, September 29 or upon the autumnal equinox.

NEPHILIM—These beings are not angels, nor are they demons. They are the offspring from the union between the Grigori and mortal women. They are said to have been giants.

The Seven Seals of the Archangels

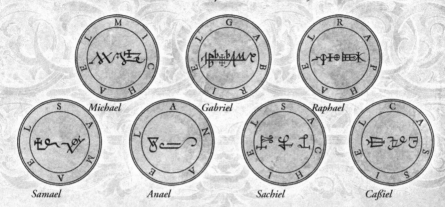

Michael · Gabriel · Raphael

Samael · Anael · Sachiel · Caßiel

RAPHAEL—His name means "God Heals," and as such he is the patron angel of physicians. He guards the Tree of Life and rescued Sarah, the daughter-in-law of Tobias, from the demon Asmodeus, who, lusting after her kept murdering her husbands on their wedding night.

RAZIEL—The "Keeper of Secrets." Raziel is said to have kept a book in which he wrote down all of God's secrets. He is to have given this book to Adam and Eve after they ate from the Tree of Knowledge. The book then passed eventually to Noah, then King Solomon.

REMEIL—One of the Archangels who is mentioned in some stories as being one of the leaders of the 200 Grigori. He is sometimes referred to as the "Thunder of God".

SANDALPHON—Before ascending to angelic form, Sandalphon was the human prophet Elijah, twin brother of Enoch, the heavenly scribe. This messenger angel delivers all human prayers to God.

SAMAEL—This angel is considered both good and evil at times. He is considered an angel of death, but is said to kill with poison, hence he is the "Venom of God." He is also called "accuser, seducer and destroyer." Some equate him with Satan, and say that it was he who tempted Eve. In some accounts he took Lilith as his wife after she left Adam.

URIEL—His name means "Fire of God." He gives prophetic warnings during times of plague or natural disaster. Uriel is credited with warning Noah of the Great Flood. He also holds the Key to the Bottomless Pit.

ZADKIEL—The "Righteousness of God" and the "Angel of Mercy." He is the patron angel of forgiveness.

Demons

Over time, many pagan gods were recast as evil demons, and even some as saints. But the word "demon" (Middle English *daemon*) did not originally have such an evil connotation. Derived from the Greek *daimon*, it simply meant a spirit that acted as a messenger between the gods and mankind. In this respect, there was no difference between the role of an angel or a demon.

The sigil of Baphomet

The Christian devil is believed to have once been a beautiful angel named Lucifer, who rebelled against his Heavenly Father and brethren. The ensuing battle between angels led to Lucifer and his followers being cast into the fires of Hell. These Fallen Angels are known as the *Grigori* in medieval lore. Throughout the Middle Ages, theologians and philosophers published manuscripts describing demons, listing their names and offices, and even providing instruction as to how to conjure them. In the sixteenth century a bishop named Peter Binsfeld paired each of the deadly sins with a demon: Lucifer (Pride), Leviathan (Envy), Satan (Wrath), Belphegor (Sloth), Mammon (Avarice), Beelzebub (Gluttony), Asmodeus (Lust).

ABADDON—Sometimes called the "Angel of the Abyss", "The Destroyer" or "Lord of Pestilence," also known as Apollyon. His appearance is that of a giant locust, or a winged warhorse with a human head and the tail of a scorpion.

AGARES—Appears in the form of an old man riding upon a crocodile and carrying a hawk on his fist. He brings back runaways, teaches languages, has the power to destroy one's dignity, and cause earthquakes. Before his Fall, he was of the order of Virtues.

AMON—Takes the appearance of a wolf with the tail of a serpent;

vomiting out of his mouth are flames. But at the command of the magician, he will assume the shape of a man with the head of a raven beset with canine fangs. He tells of things to come, can procure love and reconcile soured friendships.

ASMODEUS—A demon said to covet married women and to inspire adultery, hence his association with the sin of Lust. He can make a man invisible, and show where treasures are buried. He is described as having three heads, that of a bull, a ram and a man belching fire out of his mouth. His feet are webbed and he has the tail of a serpent. He rides

Agares   Amon   Asmodeus   Astaroth   Bael   Barbatos

Bathin   Beleth   Belial   Berith   Buer   Paimon

a dragon and carries a lance and banner. He is said to be one of the Nephilim.

ASTAROTH—Rides a dragon or a rat and carries in his left hand a viper. He is also said to expel a foul, sickening breath. When bound, he will declare willingly how he and the other angels fell, and will divulge many other secrets.

AZAZEL—The "scapegoat." As the traditional story goes, God commanded that two goats be brought forth. One was to be sacrificed to Him, the other was to carry the sins of the Israelites away into the desert, to Azazel. He was one of three angels chiefly blamed for consorting with human women during the Fall. He is also said to have been one of the leaders of the 200 Grigori. Descriptions of Azazel range from that of a beautiful, golden-haired youth, to a goat-man, to a serpent with 7 heads, 14 faces and 6 pairs of wings.

BAEL—Some say this demon is second in command to Satan. He is a king of Hell with 66 legions under his command. He appears squat, with the legs of a spider, and three heads, one of a cat, a toad, and one of a man wearing a crown. His voice is said to be very shrill and grating. He reportedly has the power to grant invisibility.

BARBATOS—Appears with four noble kings and their troops. He gives understanding of animal voices, and breaks open treasures that have been enchanted by other magicians. He is all-knowing of past and future, and reconciles friends and those in power. He was once of the order of Virtues.

BATHIN—Takes the form of a strong man with the tail of a serpent, sitting on a pale horse. He knows the virtues of herbs and precious stones, and can transport men suddenly from one country into another.

BEELZEBUB—Also called "Lord of Flies," a title he received after visiting a plague of flies upon the ancient city of Canaan. Once of the order of Seraphim, he is said to have assisted in the heavenly rebellion. He is said to inspire tyranny and lechery, demon worship, jealousy and murder, and to thrive on war. For his voracious appetites in every sinful aspect, he is the demon of Gluttony and Vanity.

BELETH—Comes riding a pale horse with trumpets playing before him. He is very furious at first appearance, but when properly exorcised—which involves a hazel stick pointed South and East and a silver ring worn on the middle finger of the left hand—he will grant "all ye love that possible may be, both of men and women."

BELIAL—It is said this demon was created next after Satan and was among the first of the Fallen to go before the Archangel Michael. He appears in the form of a beautiful angel commanding a chariot of fire. He speaks with a comely voice, declaring that he Fell first and was amongst the worthier and wiser to go before Michael and other heavenly angels. He distributes presentations and titles, grants the favor of others, and provides familiars.

BELPHEGOR—Descriptions of this demon cast two very contrasting images: a beautiful naked woman, and a monstrous bearded demon with an open mouth, horns, and sharply pointed nails. Belphegor is said to enlighten man with new discoveries, but also seduces people to laziness by tempting them with ingenious ways to avoid labor.

BERITH—Appears as a soldier clothed in red, riding on a red horse and bearing a crown of gold upon his head. He is said to bestow dignity and title, but is a notorious liar. This demon can also turn metals into gold.

BUER—A teacher of philosophy and logic. He knows the virtues of all herbs and plants. He can heal disease, and provide familiars to the magician. He is sometimes depicted as a centaur with bow and arrow. Other times he is described as having the head of a lion and five goat legs encircling his body.

LEVIATHAN—Characterized as a giant sea serpent or dragon. He is supposedly the serpent in the Garden of Eden who seduced Eve with the fruit from the Tree of Knowledge. He is the demon of Envy.

LUCIFER—According to old translations of the Bible, this is supposed to have been Satan's name before being cast out of Heaven. He is associated with the sin of Pride for his refusal to submit to the will of God. In Latin, the word "Lucifer" means "Light-Bringer" and is the name for the "Morning Star", the planet Venus as it appears at dawn.

MAMMON—The demon associated with the sin of Avarice or Greed. Also a word meaning to place extraordinary importance on wealth, or riches gained by dishonest means.

PAIMON—This demon appears in the form of a man, sitting upon a camel, with a crown on his head. He roars at his first coming, followed by a host of spirits with trumpets and cymbals. He bestows knowledge of the physical sciences, and has the power to bind a familiar to the magician. Once of the order of Dominions, he has 200 Legions of spirits under him.

SATAN—This name has traditionally come to refer to the Fallen Angel also called Lucifer. In some stories Satan and the angels Samael and Remiel are thought to be one and the same. His name also means "the accuser," which in some cultures refers to a *jinn* or evil spirit. A typical image of Satan, that of a horned goat-man with cloven hooves, is very similar in appearance to the Satyr in Greek mythology, and is oftentimes named Baphomet. In other descriptions, he looks like a dark angel with bat wings. In his human aspect he is sometimes called Mephistopheles, the demon of Faustian legend. He is the demon of Wrath.

MYSTICAL ALPHABETS

Over the past several thousand years, mankind has created numerous ways in which to record history and communicate through the written word. Magicians and sages utilized arcane symbols to scribe their spells and charms. Certain mystical alphabets were devised as a means to conceal the true meanings of magical writings, while others were believed to empower the user with unearthly abilities. Some were used as a means of divining events that had yet to unfold.

The Enochian Alphabet

The mystical alphabet known as Enochian was said to have been a gift from the angels. It was communicated to the Elizabethan astrologer and magician John Dee in the 16th century. The alchemist Edward Kelley first saw the 21 Enochian letters appear within Dee's crystal ball. Kelley later stated that angels made the letters magically appear on a page in front of him in a light yellow color. He carefully traced the shapes of the symbols with his pen before they faded from the page, preserving the forms of the Enochian letters.

The Enochian language is considered the only correct and valid language for the Enochian Calls or Keys which are used to invoke the angels. It is considered to be a powerful alphabet for spells, amulets and talismans.

The following pages contain the most renowned mystical alphabets of the world, their meanings and English language equivalents. The alphabets on these pages are based on Greek and Latin, and are readily translated into English.

The Alphabet of the Magi

The Magi were the legendary sorcerers of ancient Egypt who were said to possess the secrets of all life's mysteries. They believed that the key to the Sanctuary of Oracles was encrypted within names and numbers, and that if deciphered correctly, would reveal a person's fate as it is written in the stars. Names, phrases, wishes or spells utilizing the Alphabet of the Magi should be written in a circle. For self-enlightenment, focus on the completed circle and let your intuition guide you to note new words and phrases that form from the original letters.

A   B   C   D   E   F   G   H

I/J   K   L   M   N   O   P   Q

R   S   T   U/V/W   X   Y   Z

THEBAN SCRIPT

Also known as the Honorian Script and the Witches' Alphabet, these mysterious characters were said to be delivered by Honorius, the renowned Mage of Thebes. The letters are based on the Latin alphabet and the script was believed to be used as a cipher by ancient alchemists as a means to encode their secrets and formulas. The Theban alphabet is used primarily for magical writings and talisman inscriptions.

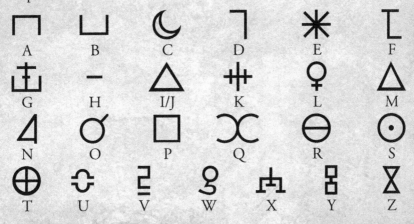

ILLUMINATI CIPHERS

Though not considered a true mystical alphabet, these characters were believed to have been used by the Bavarian Illuminati, the secret society that formed in 1776 in protest to the Christian powers of the time. The Illuminati claimed to have harnessed the ancient mystical knowledge of Mesopotamia, yet their alphabet was thought to be designed for encoding and concealing the content of their writing rather than for magical purposes. These letters are based on the Latin alphabet.

The alphabets on these pages are derived from the Jewish Kabbalah, which is based upon the premise that each of the 22 letters is a living spirit or angel. Alphabets based on Hebrew do not contain exact equivalents of English vowels, thus making it difficult to translate perfectly into English. In some cases, similar sounds are represented by one single character. For example: F and P are represented by the letter Pe. Vowels such as E, I and O are sometimes represented by the "silent" letter Ain. J and Y are represented by the letter Jod, while U, V and W are represented by the letter Vau. It is also important to note that mystical alphabets based on the Hebrew alphabet should ideally be written and read from right to left.

CELESTIAL

This text, also referred to as the Angelic alphabet, is commonly used by ceremonial magicians. It is named Celestial because the Jewish Kabbalists discerned the shapes of the celestial letters in the pattern of the stars in the heavens. Each letter shares a connection with specific stars and constellations.

Aleph	Beth	Cheth	Daleth	Ain	Pe
A	B	C/Ch	D	E/I/O	F/P
Gimel	He	Jod	Caph	Lamed	Mem
G	H	J	K	L	M
Nun	Kuff	Resh	Samech	Shin	Tau
N	Q	R	S	Sh	T
Theth	Vau	Zade	Jod	Zain	
Th	U/V/W	X	Y	Z	

MALACHIM

Meaning "of Angels" or "Regal," the Malachim alphabet is still used in the higher degrees of Freemasonry. Like the Celestial alphabet, it is based on the 22 Hebrew letters.

Aleph	Beth	Cheth	Daleth	Ain	Pe	Gimel	He	Ain
A	B	C/Ch	D	E	F	G	H	I

Jod	Caph	Lamed	Mem	Nun	Ain	Pe	Kuff
J	K	L	M	N	O	P	Q

Resh	Samech	Shin	Tau	Theth	Vau	Zade	Jod	Zain
R	S	Sh	T	Th	U/V/W	X	Y	Z

PASSING THE RIVER

This is yet a third mystical alphabet based on Hebrew script. This alphabet is used mainly by ceremonial magicians.

Aleph	Beth	Cheth	Daleth	Ain	Pe	Gimel	He	Ain
A	B	C/Ch	D	E	F	G	H	I

Jod	Caph	Lamed	Mem	Nun	Ain	Pe	Kuff
J	K	L	M	N	O	P	Q

Resh	Samech	Shin	Tau	Theth	Vau	Zade	Jod	Zain
R	S	Sh	T	Th	U/V/W	X	Y	Z

Symbols and Signs of the Mystics

Throughout the centuries, mystics of every culture have scribed countless signs and symbols, believing them to be endowed with magical powers. Many of these ancient symbols remain shrouded in mystery, for their exact meanings have been forgotten through time. The following list presents some of the more influential examples of symbols found in spiritual and mystical texts, along with their histories, adaptations, and meanings.

The Seal of King Solomon

The talisman above is just one of many such mystical seals illustrated in an ancient grimoire called *The Greater Key of Solomon*. This text as well as its counterpart, *The Goetia*, or *Lesser Key*, are purported to have been written by King Solomon. The seals are inscribed with Latin and Hebrew words and symbols signifying the names of angels, and were employed in many magical rites and as wards against evil spirits. The symbols in the four corners represent planetary angels: *Och*, angel of the Sun and healer of the sick; *Phul*, angel of the Moon and destroyer of evil water spirits; *Hagith*, angel of Venus and friend to magicians and lovers; and *Aratron*, angel of Saturn and possessor of infinite knowledge, who could turn beasts into stone and lead into gold.

Vesica Pisces—One of the most ancient of glyphs, the *vesica pisces,* represents the "divine feminine." It was used as a symbol of the goddess Venus and has been entwined into numerous other sigils. One design that incorporates this mark is the cover of the Chalice Well at Glastonbury, England. It depicts the *vesica pisces* intersected by a vertical line representing Excalibur, the sword of the legendary King Arthur, who is believed by some to be buried at Glastonbury. The wellspring at Glastonbury is considered to be one of England's most holy sites and dates back over two thousand years. Legend holds that after the crucifixion, Joseph of Arimathea traveled to Glastonbury where he secretly hid the Holy Grail.

 Triquetra—The threefold symbol called the *triquetra* (or *triqueta*) is comprised of three interlocking *vesica pisces.* In Pagan and Wiccan religions the *triquetra* represents the three stages of the Goddess: maiden, mother, and crone, or the three worldly spheres of earth, air, and water.

 Triskele—Another version of the threefold symbol, called a *triskele* (also *triskelion*), features three symmetrically placed spirals or teardrop shapes, and represents the cycles of life. These symbols were commonly employed as centerpieces in highly elaborate Celtic motifs, though variations of these patterns also appear in many other ancient cultures.

 The Horn of Odin—This symbol comprised of three stylized drinking horns arranged in a spiral pattern, represent the Norse god of war. A similar shape is used by the Japanese as an amulet called *mitsu domo* and provides triple protection against fire, flood and theft.

 Trinacria—The *trinacria,* a three-legged figure resembling a *triskele,* is a symbol of Sicily. The word means "triangular," and the three points represent the three capes of Sicily, known in ancient times as the Isle of Trinacria. The head of Medusa in the center implies the protection of the goddess Athena, while the wings of Hermes represent speed and agility. In early mythology, Medusa was the monster slain by the hero Perseus, who was aided in his task by both Athena and Hermes. The *trinacria* represents speed, power, and victory in competitive endeavors.

 **CHNOUBIS**—The *chnoubis* (also *xnoubis* or *chnoumis*) is an ancient Egyptian Gnostic icon. The lion-head represents the sun and enlightenment; the serpent body represents the earth and mans' baser impulses; the seven rays of the sun represent the seven planets known at the time. The *chnoubis* was often used on amulets for protection against poison and disease.

 NEFER—The *nefer* is an Egyptian amulet worn for good luck and was believed to endow the wearer with happiness and the vigor of youth. The word itself means "pleasant and beautiful." The symbol represents an ancient stringed musical instrument similar to a lute.

 SHEN—The *shen* was used by the ancient Egyptians to represent the life-giving force of the sun god. It was worn as an amulet to prolong human life and was frequently shown clutched in the talons of the falcon god Horus. The hieroglyph represents a coil of rope, the form of a circle symbolizing eternity, life everlasting and rejuvenation. The *shen* was believed to provide protection and was often depicted in an elongated variation surrounding the *cartouche,* which represented the names of the Pharaohs.

 TJET—The *tjet* (also *tyet* or *tet*) is an ancient Egyptian symbol, similar to the *ankh*. The *tjet* literally represents the reproductive organs of Isis, or the "Blood of Isis." This amulet is also commonly referred to as the "Buckle of Isis," and bestows upon its wearer the benevolent properties and protections of the goddess. The *tjet* can be seen in the hands of many Egyptian statues and was carved into sarcophagi as a preparation for the dead to enter the Hall of Judgment.

 ORPHIC EGG—Represented as an egg surrounded by a coiled serpent, this icon symbolizes life, rebirth, and the belief in the ancient Greek Orphic religion that the universe originated from within a silver egg. According to Orphic tradition (which is not as familiar to most as literary Greek mythology), the first emanation from this egg was the god Phanes-Dionysus, described as the personification of light. The Orphic egg shares similar concepts with the *ouroboros,* the snake that swallows its own tail and which represents the renewal of life, and the symbol of medicine known as the *caduceus.*

DJED—The *djed* is an ancient Egyptian hieroglyph representing the Tree of Life that grew around Osiris' tomb. This symbol, a called the Backbone of Osiris, was painted or carved on the base of sarcophagi, where the deceased's backbone would rest, and was considered a necessary aid in the transformation of human flesh into the spiritual form. The *djed* symbolized stability. It was also worn by the living as an amulet of regenerative power and employed for healing purposes.

MJOLNIR—This is the name given to Thor's Hammer, an ancient Norse symbol representing the legendary magical weapon that was used by Thor, god of thunder and lightning. An amulet of this design is worn for protection and symbolizes strength and rejuvenation.

SHIELD KNOT

This ancient symbol was used for thousands of years by a variety of cultures for protection and warding. The design is most often associated with Celtic and Norse tribes. An older fourfold version, called the Earth Square, is Mesopotamian in origin and is associated with protective spell.

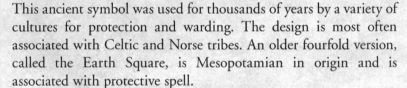

FLEUR~DE~LIS—Translated in English this means "flower of the lily" and represents purity, wisdom, and happiness and prosperity. It is widely recognized as a symbol of French nobility and was emblazoned on numerous royal crests.

ZIA—This American Indian sun symbol is found on pottery, art and other artifacts of the Zia tribes of New Mexico. Zia literally means "sun." The number four is sacred to the Zia Indians, representing the powers of nature: the four directions, seasons, and ages of man.

MOGEN DAVID—One of the oldest known religious and magical symbols is this six-sided star that represents the divine union of male and female, being composed of a water sign (female), and a fire sign (male). The traditional elemental triangles of earth, air, water, and fire are also derived from this sigil. Beginning in the Middle Ages, this came to be called the Star of David, and has been incorporated into many other seals.

OMKAR—This Hindu symbol written in ancient Sanskrit represents the sound "om" or "aum" which is said to be the primordial sound by which the earth was created. Intoned as a *mantra* during meditation, it expresses the highest form of enlightenment one can achieve.

JUNO—This sigil represents the asteroid Juno, named for the Roman goddess of marriage.

CERES—This sigil represents the asteroid Ceres, named for the Roman goddess of the harvest.

PALLAS—This sigil represents the asteroid Pallas, named for Pallas Athena, the goddess of wisdom.

MOON—This sigil represents the waxing and waning of the moon and the times of harvest.

TROLL CROSS—This amulet, formed of a ring of iron crossed at the bottom, was worn by early Scandinavian peoples as a protection against trolls and elves, for it was believed that iron and crosses were powerful wards against such creatures.

ST. BRENDAN'S CROSS—This Celtic cross, composed of four spiraling dolphins, symbolizes the sea journey of the sixth century Irish monk, Saint Brendan. Legend tells of his seven year quest for the "Land of Promise" and his return with tales of a Paradise. While there is no historical evidence of this journey, many credit him with the discovery of America.

ST. BRIDGET'S CROSS—This symbol, also known as the Bride's Cross, is traditionally woven from straw in honor of Ireland's Saint Bridget on her holiday, Candlemas, which is celebrated on the second of February. It is believed that St. Bridget was derived from the Celtic goddess of the same name, as the cross itself predates Christianity.

AEGISHJALMUR
This rune dates back to the Icelandic tribes of old. It was used as a love charm and was said to make the wearer irresistible to others.

CASTING BONES

The practice of communing with the spirit world as a means of divination has existed from earliest times. The Necromancers of ancient Egypt believed they could gain the lost wisdom of their ancestors by speaking with the dead. Druid mystics used the bones of animals to foresee the outcome of future events and to provide guidance in matters of importance. Ceremonial bones were sometimes carved or painted with words and symbols. From a leather pouch or wooden bowl, the bones were tossed into a scrying circle. The mystic would then look for patterns in the placement of the bones to divine the future.

THE ORACLE OF THE BONES

Think of a question concerning a specific aspect of your life and focus your mind on it. Select any one of the Bone Patterns in the circle by placing your finger upon it. Pick a number between 10 and 30 then move your finger clockwise around the circle for the same number of symbols. The symbol you land on announces your oracle. Consult your oracle for advice concerning your question by using the chart on the following pages.

LIBERA ANIMAS OMNIUM FIDELIUM DEFUNCTORUM DE POENIS OBSCURUM

Solitude—This pattern indicates individuality and self-reliance. You have the power within yourself to conquer any adversity, but you must travel your current path alone. Look to your inner strengths to resolve your present situation.

Union—This pattern signifies a meeting of minds and hearts. It denotes a balance of needs and a solid relationship. A collective effort will be rewarding. In matters of the heart, this pattern is a sign of harmony and passion.

Conflict—This pattern represents a clash of opposing forces. Your ideas will be met with resistance. Prepare for a difficult struggle. Use reason and diplomacy to attain a compromise, but if necessary, be prepared to summon and utilize all your strengths to achieve your goal.

Serenity—This pattern foretells of physical and emotional tranquility derived from inner reflection and indicates a positive outcome of any present dilemma. Set your worries aside and take time to relax and enjoy your surroundings.

Conquest—This positive omen denotes triumph over adversity through the force of mental and physical strengths. You are destined to succeed in your endeavors, and any opposition encountered will be easily overcome as long as you remain steadfast and focused on your goal.

Renewal—This pattern represents a second chance at missed opportunities or a renewal in affairs of the heart. This is also a good omen that foretells of rejuvenation and healing. Look to the past for answers to your current situation.

Patience—This pattern symbolizes constraint and discipline. Take the time to plan carefully before leaping into action. Don't act on impulse. Good things come to those who wait, but take care not to mistake patience for procrastination.

Wisdom—This pattern indicates the acquisition and use of knowledge. You will be tested and may require advice from someone who possesses more experience and wisdom. Study your current situation carefully so that you can determine how to use your knowledge and experience to achieve your goals.

Journey—This pattern indicates travel or the arrival of news from afar. Keep an open mind and be prepared to change course to reach your goal. In matters of the heart, this indicates that some distance may soon come between you and your partner.

 Loss—This pattern signifies a setback and personal strife. It may also represent the loss of a loved one. Be prepared to rethink your strategy or change course to attain your goal. Look to close friends for consolation.

 Reward—This is a positive omen of fulfillment and material gain. Your hard work, patience and perseverance will soon pay off. It also symbolizes the reward for overcoming obstacles in your path. Good fortune will shine upon you.

 Sacrifice—This pattern indicates that you will have to surrender something you cherish to attain your heart's desire. You may have to relinquish that which holds you back from attaining your goal. Stay focused on your main priority.

 Deception—This sign indicates that the truth is being concealed and things are not as they appear. Your secrets are safe, but be careful who you trust. Take a closer look at your surroundings to discover what lies beneath the surface.

 Strength—This is a sign of determination, extreme confidence, and vitality. You will have a winning, competitive spirit in matters of business and romance. Be forceful, remain focused and believe in yourself and you will succeed.

 Intuition—This represents insight, imagination and artistic creativity. This pattern also signifies occult abilities and things shrouded in mystery. You are being guided and protected by higher powers. Follow and trust your own instincts.

 Fruition—This is a symbol of personal achievement regarding the ultimate completion of an idea or dream. It also signifies prosperity, fertility and childbirth. Your endeavors culminate and blossom, and your plans are fully realized. It is time to enjoy the fruits of your labors and set new goals for the future.

The Art of
Alchemy

The mystical art of Alchemy was the predecessor of the modern science of chemistry and was handed down through the millennia from Egypt and Arabia to Greece and Rome, and finally to western and central Europe. The word is derived from the Arabic phrase "al-kimia," which translates to mean "of Egypt," and refers to the fertile Nile valley and the mysterious rites of the ancient Egyptians.

CENTRUM MUNDI
COCATENATUM

IGNIS · AER · AQUA · TERRA

SATURNI · MARTIS · SOLIS · MERCURY · LUNAE · VENERIS · IOUIS

Through Daphne
fly from Phoebus
bright, yet shall they
both be one. And if
you understand this
right, you have our
hidden Stone. For
Daphne she is
faire and white, but
Volatile is she.
Phoebus a fixed
God of might, and
red as blood is he.
Daphne is a Water
Nymph, and hath of
Moysture store.

Which Phoebus
doth consume with
heate, and dryes her
very sore. They being
dryed into one, of
christall fhend must
drinke, till they be
brought to a white
Stone. Wash with
Virgin's Milke, so
longe intill they flow
as wax, and in fume
you can see, then
have you all you
neede to wishe, and
then thankful be.

Meridies   Occidens

PRIMA MATERIA
Mineralia
Animalia   Vegetabilia

Oriens   Septentrio

QUINTA ESSENTIA

The Art of Alchemy

The basic goals of the alchemists were threefold: to discover the secret of life, to perfect the transmutation of metals, and to find or create a mystical artifact known as The Philosopher's Stone. To the medieval alchemist's mind the different base metals were but the same original substance in varying degrees of purity, gold being the purest of all.

The Philosopher's Stone

Since about the 3rd century alchemists have taken extreme measures in order to discover the existence of this elusive artifact. The Philosopher's Stone, which was reportedly a compound of substances requiring lengthy and tedious preparations, was said to have the power to change large quantities of inexpensive base metals into gold, and that only a minuscule amount was required in order to make the transformation. This mysterious and secret substance was also exalted as the *Elixir Vitae* ("Elixir of Life") and could supposedly heal and prevent all illness. Kings throughout the ages have employed alchemists in the hopes of acquiring great wealth and immortality. Many crafty conjurors gained the king's favor with promises of fantastic power and riches, and the possibility that such a substance

could actually exist certainly afforded the alchemist a place to work, time to study, and money to purchase equipment and materials. And although it is likely that a few charlatans were simply biding their time at court, a good many alchemists used the opportunity to secretly work toward other more humane goals.

The Philosopher's Stone, also called the "Stone of Knowledge" and the *Prima Materia* ("Original Building Materials of Creation"), is considered an allegory for the acquisition of knowledge, and those who recognized this made priceless contributions to the betterment of humankind. By the 18th century, alchemists had moved beyond superstition and had brought to light many wonders in the arts of science and medicine.

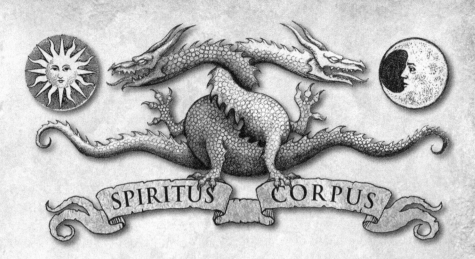

SPIRITUS ◆ CORPUS

Throughout the medieval centuries, the advancement of science was suppressed and alchemists were persecuted by religious zealots who believed alchemy to be a form of black magic. In the early days of alchemy, the astronomical signs of the planets as well as the astrological signs of the Zodiac were used as alchemical symbols, but during these dark ages when any scientific knowledge was considered to be a mortal sin, each alchemist invented his own secret symbols and glyphs to conceal the true nature of his experiments. What follows are the most well known symbols used by the ancient alchemists.

The Seven Metals

From antiquity up until the 18th century, alchemists recognized only seven base metals.

⊙   Gold (Sun)

☽   Silver (Moon)

♀   Copper (Venus)

♂   Iron (Mars)

♄   Lead (Saturn)

♃   Tin (Jupiter)

☿   Quicksilver (Mercury)

Seasons

Ɛ   Spring

Ӿⅴ   Summer

Ỡ   Autumn

ᴨ   Winter

THE CLASSIC ELEMENTS

The ancient Greek and Roman alchemists recognized four principal "elements," properties of which were attributed to a particular substance. The alchemists of the time further believed that there was a correlation between practical science and spiritual beliefs. This idea also crossed over into astronomy and astrology, hence, the signs of the Zodiac share properties of the classic elements. Following are the four elements, their phases and associated Zodiac signs.

▽ *Earth*—The phase of blackening, called *melanosis,* represented by earth, which is associated with Taurus, Virgo, and Capricorn.

▽ *Water*—The phase of whitening, called *leucosis,* represented by water, which is associated with Cancer, Scorpio, and Pisces.

△ *Air*—The phase of yellowing, called *xanthosis,* represented by air, which is associated with Gemini, Libra, and Aquarius.

△ *Fire*—The phase of reddening, called *iosis,* represented by fire, associated with Aries, Leo, and Sagittarius.

♃ *Quinta Essentia*—This was considered to be the "Fifth Element," another term for *aether,* the substance of which the heavenly bodies were composed. This was a philosophical element and was sometimes eluded to as being the substance of the Philosopher's Stone. In a baser sense, it is the *quintessence,* or highly concentrated form of a substance.

TERRA   AQUA   AER   IGNIS

Elements & Minerals

An *element* is a material which is the building block for many other substances. Elements are typically classified as being metallic or non-metallic. An *alloy* is a combination of two or more elements, at least one of which is a metal. An *ore* is a mineral which contains a metal, and must be mined in order to extract the metal. Metals usually found in ore include: copper, lead, silver and zinc. A *mineral* is a solid chemical compound that has a *crystalline* structure, such as table salt. Liquids and gases are not considered minerals, but they may carry minerals. Rocks are not minerals, but may also contain minerals or metals within veins or seams. The following is a list of elements and minerals, as they were known to the medieval alchemists, their properties and common uses.

♆ **Antimony**—A bluish-white metallic element that was used as early as 3000 BC, prized for its fine casting qualities. It was used as a medicine and a cosmetic due to its lustrous appearance. However, antimony is highly toxic. In small doses, antimony causes headache, dizziness and depression. Larger doses cause death within days.

⚒ **Arsenic**—A notorious poison known to alchemists for thousands of years. Although primarily employed for pest control, it was also a favorite weapon of murder. Arsenic was often included in the making of bronze alloy as a hardener.

♁ **Bismuth**—A brittle metallic element with a pinkish hue and an iridescent tarnish. It was used in producing malleable irons, and was often mistaken for tin or lead. When burned in the open air it produces a brilliant blue flame and yellow fumes.

♋ **Borax**—This is a compound of the element boron. Borax is formed naturally from the evaporation of saline lakes (lakes having a significant content of salt, found in arid regions). When dissolved in water it is useful as a disinfectant, detergent, and water softener. It is also used in the manufacture of ceramics, paint, glass, and coated paper, and as a flux in welding.

♀ **Bronze & Brass**—Bronze includes a range of alloys of copper, usually with zinc, tin or nickel. Bronze resists corrosion, especially from seawater, making tools, weapons and armor which were harder and more durable than their stone and copper predecessors. Brass is the term for an alloy specifically made of copper and zinc.

Calx—Also known as chalk, calx was mined in the form of limestone, which was used in ancient times for building material and as a fertilizer for fields. Medicinally, chalk was, and is still today, used as an antacid for its content of calcium carbonate.

Cinnabar—A crystal, similar to quartz, with a scarlet-red color, also known as Vermilion. Cinnabar was mined by the Roman Empire for its content of the element mercury, and has remained the main ore of mercury throughout the centuries.

Cobalt—This metallic element is named after the German *kobold,* an evil spirit believed to inhabit caves. It was so named by copper miners because it was poisonous and considered a pollutant of the other metal ores which they sought. Cobalt was primarily used in glassmaking to give a rich blue color to the glass. It is also used as pigment for paints, varnishes, inks, and enamels.

Magnesium—A silvery-white, lightweight metallic element found in deposits of minerals such as magnesite and dolomite. The pure powdered form is highly flammable; it heats and ignites when exposed to air and burns with a blinding white flame. When hydrated it is called "milk of magnesia" and has the medicinal property of a laxative. When boiled down and condensed into a sulfate, it is used as a therapeutic bath known as Epsom salts.

Nickel—A metallic element that can be traced back as far as 3500 BC, when it was used as an additive to some bronze alloys. Minerals containing nickel were used in glassmaking to give a green hue. Today, nickel is chiefly used in the making of stainless steel, an alloy of iron and nickel.

Pewter—This metal alloy of tin and lead was most commonly used during the Middle Ages for drinking tankards, plates, cutlery and jewelry.

Phosphorus—Alchemists often used light as a symbol of the spirit, and were especially interested in light that seemed to be trapped in matter such as the element phosphorus. One medieval experiment proposed to use the tails of glow worms as a portable light source, a "perpetual fire."

Platinum—This metal was called *platina* or "little silver" by the Spaniards, who generally regarded it as an unwanted impurity in the silver they were mining. It was often discarded because it was impossible to melt by the standards of the day. Harder than silver or gold, and resistant to corrosion or tarnishing, platinum is considered today to be even more valuable than gold.

⊖ *Salt*—A mineral produced by the evaporation of seawater, brine-rich lakes, or by mining rock salt. Salt is absolutely essential to life, and was such a valuable commodity in ancient times that it was used as a form of payment. Salt was as important to ancient commerce as gold trading.

⊬ *Steel*—An alloy of iron and the non-metallic element carbon. Ancient tools, swords and armor made of steel would still rust, yet were lighter and stronger than those made of solid iron.

⊕ *Talc*—This mineral formed from magnesium was used for cosmetic purposes, for its fragrance retention, luster, purity, softness, and whiteness. A coarse grayish-green form of talc is called soapstone and was used for making many household implements due to the ease with which it could be carved.

♰ *White Lead*—This white powder is similar to zinc oxide, but it contains lead. It was used in paint pigments since earliest times, and is now known to be poisonous if ingested or inhaled over long periods of time.

♯ *Zinc*—A metallic element which has been used for centuries in alloys such as brass to prevent corrosion. Goods made of zinc have been found in Palestine dating back as early as 1000-1400 BC, and in prehistoric Transylvania. The medicinal properties of zinc are well known to promote healing. Zinc white (zinc oxide) is used as a white pigment in watercolors.

CAUSTIC SUBSTANCES

A caustic substance is one that "eats away" or chemically burns other materials. Many of these are considered a chemical compound, a substance formed from two or more elements. This includes sulfate chemical salts which are different that mineral salts, as well as acids that are produced by combining sulfates with other substances.

⚗ *Alum*—A crystallized sulfate derived from the evaporation and condensation of vapors from heated metal, wood or clay. Alum has numerous applications, but was primarily used in early history for dyeing and tanning, papermaking and water purification.

♈ *Aqua Regia*—This compound of the element nitrogen (specifically the combination of nitric acid with hydrochloric acid) was celebrated for its ability to dissolve gold and platinum.

Ⓘ Nitre—Also called "saltpeter," (from medieval Latin *sal petrae* meaning "stone salt"), was a mineral compound (potassium nitrate) mainly used as a preservative in the curing of meats. Medicinally it acts as a diuretic and it is also employed as a fertilizer.

Ⓟ Potash—This is made from the ashes of burnt wood. Potash has been used since antiquity, chiefly as a fertilizer. Caustic potash, or lye, was the chief ingredient used in soap making and was made by steeping the wood ashes in water for a long time.

Ⓩ Quicklime—This is produced by the thermal decomposition of limestone, and was one of the first chemical reactions discovered by man. It is very caustic to bare skin. Also called slaked lime, this is used as a hardening agent in mortar and plaster. Lime is also found in marble, chalk, bones, and shells.

Ⓢ Sulfur—When burnt, sulfur emits a blue flame and a suffocating stench. This was commonly referred to as "brimstone." It was used widely for pest control, and is a key ingredient in gunpowder.

Ⓥ Vitriol—This was the medieval name for sulfuric acid, a highly corrosive agent known to alchemists as early as the 9th century. The vitriol salts were extracted from the water runoff that collected inside mines; the sulfates formed naturally by the process of evaporation on the wet minerals.

Ⓞ Oil of Vitriol—This concentrated form of sulfuric acid is the "essence" of vitriol, so-called for its glassy, oily appearance.

Alchemical Processes

Ⓐ Amalgamation—The formation of an alloy of mercury and any other metal except iron, which cannot be combined with the element of mercury.

Ⓐ Annealing—A process of heating and slow cooling in order to toughen and reduce brittleness in the material, such as in ironworking or glassmaking.

Ⓑ Boiling—Heating a substance until it changes from a liquid to a gaseous state. It was discovered that different substances required varying amounts of added heat to reach the stage of boiling, the "boiling point."

♃ Calcination—The breaking down of a substance by fierce heating and burning usually in an open crucible.

♄ Composition—The joining together of two elements to create a new substance.

♅ Dissolution—The dissolving of a solid substance into a liquid state.

♓ Distillation—The separation of a component from a substance by heating so that the component separates as a vapor, which is condensed, either as a liquid or crystal, in a cooler part of the apparatus.

♈ Ebullition—The effervescence produced by fermentation.

♋ Fermentation—Described as the rotting of a substance, usually of an organic nature, often accompanied by the release of gas bubbles. This is one of the first known processes discovered and practiced by mankind, dating as far back as 7000 years.

♉ Lixiviation—The process of leaching; to separate a soluble substance (that which can be dissolved by liquid) from one which is insoluble, usually by soaking it in a solvent, such as water or alcohol.

♊ Precipitation—To separate a substance from a solution. The solid precipitate descends to the bottom of the flask.

♌ Pulverization—The breaking down of a substance to smaller fragments through repeated striking with a blunt instrument, such as a hammer, or mallet.

♍ Purification—The process of removing impurities, as from metals, oil, sugar, etc. It is a general term which may include a series of processes.

♎ Putrefaction—The rotting of a substance, often under a prolonged period of time and by a gentle, moist heat. Usually the matter becomes black.

♏ Sublimation—When a material is heated and gives off a vapor, thereby changing directly from a solid state to a gaseous state without becoming liquid. The vapor then condenses on the cooler part of the flask to be collected as a solid powder.

⊹ Torrefaction—To subject a substance to a scorching heat, so as to drive off volatile ingredients; to roast, as with ores.

℞ Recipe—This word is derived from the Latin *recipere,* meaning an instruction "to take," as of a mixture or compound, usually with a list of measured ingredients and set directions for their use and application. The symbol is the original prescription (Rx) symbol. Recipes often included specifics about star alignment and seasonal periods.

Weights & Measures

These units of apothecary weight are different than today's pharmaceutical standards.

℔ Pound = 12 ounces

℥ Ounce = 8 drams

ʒ Dram = 3 scruples

Ɔ Scruple = 20 grains

āā Ana = "an equal measure"

Working Materials

Ⓧ Glass   Ⓐ Crystal   ⚐ Stone   ⚏ Wood

Instruments

Ⓤ Cribble—A coarse sieve or screen through which solid substances would be sifted in order to reduce the size of the particles.

∇ Crucible—A bucket-like container used for heating metal in a furnace. The crucible must be of a harder metal than that which is being melted.

∿ Filter—A fine cloth or screen through which solid substances are separated from liquids.

Receiver—A container with a long tubular neck used for collecting a distilled substance.

Retort—A closed container with a long tubular neck, used during the distillation and sublimation processes.

Ⓧ Still—This contraption combined a furnace with various tubes and flasks. A substance would be heated into a liquid or vapor, where it would then be distilled.

Common Ingredients & Uses

Aqua Vitae—This translates to the "water of life." It is distilled alcohol, as in hard liquor, and was not used just for drinking. Its main purpose to the alchemist was as an extracting agent.

Eggshells—Valued for their calcium content and used as a fertilizer.

Ginger—A food spice and an effective treatment for nausea.

Hartshorn—The antler of a hart (a male red deer) used as a source of ammonia for smelling salts.

Honey—This sweet product was highly valued because it does not spoil, and was therefore used as a food preservative. It is also the main ingredient in mead.

Oil—The distilled concentrate of a given substance, which includes plant, animal and mineral oils.

Wine—Discovered in jars dating as far back as 7000 years ago in ancient Babylon. It is believed that ancient Egyptians practiced the art of winemaking, procuring grapes through trade since they never grew there. The art of winemaking spread throughout the Mediterranean in Greece and Rome and later to western Europe, rivaling beer as the drink of choice. Wine was important in religion, commerce, and in all aspects of life.

Vinegar—From the Old French word *vinaigre* meaning "sour wine." Vinegar was used primarily as a food preservative, as in "pickling." Malt vinegar, made from aged barley, is used as a condiment for food, while white vinegar, made by distilling malt vinegar, is used chiefly as a cleansing agent.

Sugar—Long known throughout tropical regions, sugar cane was chewed for its sweetness but the cane could not be grown in the northern hemisphere, and so was acquired through trade. Refining was later developed in the Middle East, India and China. The refined sugar crystals eventually came to Europe with the Moors. The Crusaders brought sugar home with them after their holy campaigns.

Tartar—This substance forms during the fermentation process. Tartar crystallizes in wine casks, and upon further purification, yields *cream of tartar*, which is used as a leavening agent in baking powders.

LOVE SPELLS

CHARMS AND BINDINGS

Since the dawn of time,
men and women have
sought ways to attract and
invoke passion in the
opposite sex. The following
pages encompass some of
the ancient practices for
weaving spells of attraction
and love. Always
remember, above all, there
is no stronger magic than
that of true love.

PASSION · DEVOTION · HONESTY

MARS

EROS

AMORE

ISIS

VENUS

KAPHE KASTA NON KAPHETA ET PUBLICA FILII URE IGNE SANCTI SPIRITUS RENIS NOSTROS ET COR NOSTRUM SINS OMNIBUS SUIS

ROMANCE

FIDELITY

HARMONY

DESIRE

Aphrodisiacs

This term is derived from Aphrodite, the Greek goddess of love, who sprang forth from the sea on an oyster shell. Many organic ingredients are considered natural aphrodisiacs. They can be procured from the garden or nearby woodland, though some should be harvested at particular times. Various herbs and roots may also be found in metaphysical shops and health food stores. Some items may be worn or carried in a small satchel, others may be placed around the home, while some charms are to be placed near the person who you wish to influence.

Foods that fuel the fires of love include apple, avocado, celery, and cherry, as well as the traditional oyster. Serve peaches, pears, papaya or strawberries to a desired one to win his or her heart or to intensify feelings of love. Herbs and spices that promote passion include cinnamon, coriander, garlic, lemongrass, mint, nutmeg, parsley, sesame, and ginseng tea. To inspire lust, grind seven grains of coriander, stir into a glass of red wine, and share the potion with a lover.

The Color of Passion—Wearing the color red on Friday is said to ensure a passionate weekend. Red candles, roses and gems such as garnet and ruby are all employed in ritual to inspire passion and lust. A letter, written in red ink and sealed with a kiss will stimulate the romantic spirit of the one you desire. Place rose petals and fresh rosemary leaves in your shoes to make romance blossom wherever you go.

Passionate Perfumes—Orris root, jasmine, vanilla, hibiscus, gardenia, violet, lavender, patchouli and sandalwood all act as aphrodisiacs and are used in ritual to attract lovers. These seductive scents may be added to a bath, used as an anointing oil, or burned as incense to incite lust. Rosewater baths will soften the skin and will especially soften your lover's heart.

To Attract New Love

Apple—This fruit is a symbol of Venus. A charm for attraction can be prepared as a potpourri by slicing the apple into thin sections and allowing it to dry, then adding some cinnamon stick and oak bark. It may be worn against the heart in a red satchel to elicit the attentions of someone you desire. The potpourri may also be simmered or placed around your home to enchant your surroundings with an atmosphere of passion.

Orange Pomander—Oranges and cloves are both strong symbols of love due to their sweet tastes and scents. Making this charm to attract love is simple: Take a fresh orange and stud it with cloves. Using a red ribbon, tie the orange with a stick of cinnamon and hang this charm in your closet, allowing it to render its magic in secrecy.

Myrtle—Ancient Greeks and Romans used this flower in garlands to hang in the home. A favorite of Venus, its properties preserve youth and promote love and friendship. May also be worn in a satchel.

Sweet Bugle—Crush and sprinkle the dried flowers and leaves of this plant around your bedroom to attract a new lover.

Periwinkle—This delicate flower brings a promise of love. Leave to dry until brittle, then grind into a fine powder using a stone mortar. Sprinkle the powder in the path of the person you desire to draw their heart to yours.

Sandalwood—This scent enforces the strength of a wish. Burn a stick of sandalwood incense while reciting the following verse, invoking the names of the Roman god and goddess of love: *"Eros, Venus, I beseech thee, my heart's desire deliver to me."* Then repeat the name of the person you desire three times.

Lovage Root—This root should be wrapped thrice with a red ribbon and worn near the heart to attract a new lover.

John the Conqueror Root—This root contains magical properties and brings to its owner friendship and good will.

Adam & Eve Root—This root is common to native orchids. It is so named due to the growth habit of the bulbs. The leaf and flower arise from the current season's growth, called Eve, while the previous year's bulb is called Adam (from which Eve sprang forth) and is still present and full of seeds. Wrap the pair in pink silk and carry them to attract love. The roots may also be carried separately by two lovers (Eve for the female, Adam for the male) to ensure the faithfulness of each person.

♥ *Spell of Attraction*—If you have your heart set on someone in particular, but they have yet to notice you, first find out where they live. Prepare a mixture of rose hips, crushed periwinkle, and dill seed. Sprinkle a bit of it beneath his or her bedroom window at the hour of midnight. Leave a trail of this mixture, casting a pinch at each crossroad or turn until you reach the threshold of your own home, to draw the person's affections to you.

♥ *The Power of Words*—To woo someone with words, first drink a glass of water with a slice of lemon and a sprig of mint. It will make your softest whispers sound like sweet music to the one you desire.

To Ensure Fidelity and Devotion

Eryngo—This flower (also called Sea Holly) was worn by the brides in ancient Greece on their wedding day to ensure fidelity in their marriage.

Marjoram—This herb is ruled by Venus. One seeking a long-lasting relationship should sprinkle this in all the corners of their house.

Orange Blossoms—Mix with anise seed, orris root, and rose hips and wear in a sachet close to the heart to bring longevity to a relationship. Blossoms added to a bride's flower bouquet will bring good luck to newlyweds.

Meadowsweet—Most sacred to the Druids, this flower is often used to decorate one's altar when mixing love charms or performing love spells. Sometimes called brideswort, this is a favorite flower for bridal garlands. Grow near the home to keep a couple together for at least seven years.

Vervain—Ruled by Venus, this herb may be carried on one's person if seeking a lasting love and a promise of fidelity.

Trusted Gems—To ensure faithfulness in a new relationship, give your lover jewelry made from either peridot or green jade.

Foods of Fidelity—Some of the foods that promote fidelity include lettuce, olives, and parsley. A wife may dust her upper body with powdered basil to keep her husband faithful. Licorice root may be added to love sachets and used in spells to ensure commitment and fidelity.

♥ **Spell of Devotion**—Under the guise of foretelling the future, gaze into your lover's eyes, then taking their hand in yours, and with a compelling voice speak aloud the following phrase: *"Kaphe, Kasita, non Kapheta et publica filii omnibus suis."* He or she will be completely devoted to you.

♥ **Spell of Binding**—Pluck three hairs from your head and obtain three from the one you love. Plait the hairs together and cast them onto a fire along with three rose petals. While it burns, recite this prayer: *"Ure igne sancti Spiritus renes nostros et cor nostrum, Domine, Amen."* Your hearts will be forever bound.

♥ **Hearts Entwined**—To be certain that your lover is faithful while you are separated, draw two interlocked hearts on a piece of lavender colored paper. Write your name inside one of the hearts and your lover's name in the other. Burn the paper beneath a full moon and allow the ashes to scatter. As long as your own heart does not stray, your lover will remain as faithful as you are.

♥ **Faithful Crystals**—Take two small quartz crystals and place them on the ground together so they touch one another. Leave them out all night beneath a full moon, then give one to your lover to carry or wear while you keep the other. As long as you each carry the crystals, you will enjoy a faithful relationship that no amount of time or distance can hinder.

To Impassion a Lover

Rose—This flower is a symbol of Venus. Rose-scented oil may be added to bath water to attract a lover. When preparing for a passionate liaison also sprinkle a few grains of dill seed into the bath for added charisma. Rose petals strewn across a bed promise tenderness in matters of love.

Lavender—The aroma of this fragrant flower has power over dreams. Place a sprig beneath your pillow before going to sleep. If you dream of the person you desire, your wishes for that person will come true. Place it beneath the pillow of a lover and he or she will dream only of you.

Violet—A favorite of the goddess Venus, this flower has a seductive aroma. Bathe with violet-scented oils or use soaps with this fragrance to increase your allure. Gently caress your loved one under the chin with one of the soft petals to ensure tender embraces. A flowering plant in the home brings the added favor of good spirits and guards against illness.

Juniper berries—May be dried and strung to attract a lover, and are often carried to increase male potency.

Honey—This sweet substance can be a strong aphrodisiac. Spread lightly upon your lips, then kiss your lover and expect a passionate response.

Deer Horn and Hooves—Crushed deer horn is considered to be a powerful aphrodisiac and is used in love spells. The hooves are a powerful amulet, garnering for its owner sexual appeal.

Ambergris—This substance is used to draw out and heighten the scent of natural pheromones. It is used primarily by the perfume industry, so look for this ingredient when choosing a fragrance.

♥ **A Bewitching Bath**—Add five peeled oranges and a handful of fresh mint leaves to your bathwater. Squeeze the juice from the oranges and rub the mint leaves into your hair and anoint your skin. Rinse, but do not soap off. Allow your body and hair to air-dry. When you later cuddle with your lover, the scent will make you irresistible. Washing your face and hair with chamomile tea is another recipe for attracting a lover.

♥ **Will-o Will I Wed?** On New Year's Eve throw your shoe into a willow tree. If it doesn't catch and stay in the branches the first time, you have eight more tries. If you succeed in trapping your shoe in the tree you will be wed within the year.

FERTILITY CHARMS

Fertile Foodstuffs—A variety of nuts, grapes, poppy seeds, and sunflower seeds are all recommended for those seeking to conceive children. Place fresh rosemary herb under the bed when trying to conceive. Raspberries are a love inducing food, and the leaves are carried by expectant mothers to alleviate the pains of childbirth. Dried orange peel is a common ingredient in potpourri love and fertility charms.

Harvesting Health—To ensure a healthy birth, one apple and a good deal of positive energy is required. Cut the apple in half. The mother-to-be should eat one half while envisioning a happy, healthy child. The other half should be rubbed over the mother's belly, while envisioning any sickness being drawn out and into the apple. Bury the tainted half (with seeds) in the ground. If a tree grows from the apple seeds, the child will grow to be strong and firmly grounded, and will never know hunger.

To Rekindle Lost Passion

Magnolia—Gather the leaves from the blossoming plant and spread them beneath the mattress to arouse passion in a lover who has become indifferent. Wear this flower or a perfume made of this flower to keep a lover from straying.

Heartsease—Place a bit of this herb (part of the violet family) on the soles of your lover's shoes without his or her knowledge to soften their heart and fill it with tenderness for you.

Rosemary—Add this herb to food dishes prepared for your lover to encourage his or her sexual appetite.

Mandrake Root—This legendary plant (*Mandragora*, of the nightshade family) is a powerful ingredient in many spells and brings sexual potency to its owner. When placed under the pillow of a lover who has become indifferent, that person will soon become passionate again. The mandrake root should preferably be harvested by the light of the moon to have the strongest effect in magical spells.

To Bring The Return Of A Lost Lover

Spikenard—Brew this herb (part of the ginseng family) as a tea and sprinkle over the photograph of a lover who has wandered.

Cloves—Clasp a handful of crushed cloves tightly in your fist while envisioning the one you love. He or she will feel compelled to visit you. The aroma of cloves resurrects memories of passion. Cloves may be carried in a satchel to attract love.

Damiana—Soak this herb in white wine for three hours, then sprinkle the mixture at the threshold of your door. Do this every evening at sunset for 21 days.

♥ *Heart's Desire*—This spell should be prepared first by mixing together powdered rose and lavender incense with damiana herb, which is to be placed in an incense burner or cauldron. Next, anoint yourself with a few drops of rose oil, then cast a magic circle. Light a red candle, turn clockwise in a complete circle, then set it to your left. Light a green candle, turn in the same direction to cast the circle again, then set it on your right. Light a pink candle, and hold it while you recite the following invocation three times:

> *"Venus, goddess of desire, I pray and ask of thee—*
> *Light the pathway to my heart, And guide true love to me."*

Finally, blow out the candles and light the herb and incense and allow it to burn through the night while you dream. Love will soon find its way to you.

♥ **Mending a Broken Heart**—Cut two small heart shapes from a piece of red velvet. Place some crushed rose petals sprinkled with lavender oil between the two pieces of material. Then, using a single length of golden thread, sew the two halves together with the rose petals inside. Carry this charm with you wherever you go and your sorrow will soon fade away. Geranium and patchouli scents are also said to help ease the pain of a broken heart.

♥ **Tears of Healing**—To make a new romance blossom after experiencing heartbreak, wipe your tears on a silk cloth. Hold the cloth against your bare chest, directly over your heart and recite the following poem:
"Love was gifted, then forsaken, With these words may it yet awaken—Release me from this pain I bear, And bestow me with a love to share."

LOVE AMULETS

The use of amulets dates back to ancient times. They are usually fashioned by hand, using natural elements such as clay, wood, stone or metal as a base. Some have even become common symbols of love, though they still hold great power when used reverently.

The Beryl Stone—This is a sea-green stone, which if carved with the likeness of a frog and set in gold, will gain for its wearer the affection of anyone who touches it or who is touched by it. When dipped into water, it brings to the owner the friendship of all who drink.

Emerald—This precious gem ensures tenderness in lovemaking and may be used to divine a truth or falsehood in regards to a lover's vow. This stone also preserves chastity in virgins.

Moonstone or Selenite—This is a stone which awakens passion and promotes fidelity between lovers.

Copper—This metal, as well as the color green, is ruled by the sign of Venus. Jewelry made of copper may be worn to increase sexual potency and prevent one's love life from wilting with age. Set with a green stone to strengthen its powers.

Ruby—This precious stone aids in all matters of love. It is especially potent as a love amulet when fashioned into the shape of a heart.

The Jade Butterfly—A stone of jade fashioned into the figure of a butterfly will bestow a blessing of love upon the wearer.

The Angel Amulet—This amulet is written in the alphabet of the angels. This parchment is to be scribed in red ink, then rolled and secured with a ring of gold, and kept on one's person.

Venus Stone—Pink quartz is a symbol of Venus. An amulet made of this material brings love to its wearer, promotes the prospect of marriage, and fertility.

The Talisman of Venus—Scribe this talisman on both sides of a piece of parchment, though preferably it should be engraved into copper. To consecrate the amulet, expose it to an aroma of violets and roses burned with olive wood in an earthenware vessel. This must be done on a Friday, as this is the day consecrated to Venus. Carry the amulet in a sachet of green or pink silk or wear it as a pendant close to your heart to attract love or to preserve harmony in a relationship. If an enemy drinks liquid in which the talisman has been dipped, that person's hatred will turn to affection and devotion.

Mars & Venus—When these two planetary signs are intertwined the resulting symbol represents the physical union of man and woman. An amulet depicting this symbol may be worn to increase sexual potency, ensure fertility and bring strength to any relationship.

Fehe—This ancient runic symbol is used to attract love. Scribe this mark with henna or vegetable dye on your right palm to gain friendship, or on your inner right thigh if it is a more amorous love you wish to attract.

A SIGN OF TRUST—The sigil of Juno, named for the Roman goddess of marriage, should be drawn on a piece of parchment or inscribed at the end of a letter that your loved one reads to ensure that their heart will remain committed and true to you.

AEGISHJALMUR is a rune that dates back to the Icelandic tribes of old. It was used as a love charm to make the wearer irresistible to others. Worn as a pendant, or tattooed on one's body this mystical symbol is believed to enhance the wearer's personal aura.

THE SEAL OF HAGITH—This ancient symbol represents the Angel of Venus and grants true friendship and love. Draw this seal on a piece of parchment and place it behind a framed photograph of the one you desire to attract. It may also be used as a seal on letters sent to the one you love.

THE HEART—This is a traditional symbol of love and friendship. It is worn to bring love and is especially lucky when fashioned of a red stone such as a ruby, carnelian, or garnet.

CUPID'S ARROW—The practice of writing your name or initials along with those of your heart's desire inside the drawing of a heart pierced by an arrow is an age old childhood custom, but it is believed that this simple talisman will appeal to the Roman god Cupid, who's arrows delivered love to mortals.

THE UNICORN—This mythical beast is a strong symbol of fertility and sexuality. Amulets made of silver or white enamel formed into this figure or engraved with it are worn by those wishing to increase their sexual magnetism.

DREAMS, OMENS & PROPHECY

DREAM LOVER—To see your true love in your dreams, place a drop of jasmine oil on your pillow before you go to sleep at night.

SONGBIRDS & RAINBOWS—If you hear a songbird singing outside your bedroom window as the sun rises, you will see your true love sometime that day. Rainbows are also believed to guide you toward finding your soul mate. If you see a rainbow in the sky, it means that your true love lies in that direction.

Divining Daisy—Plucking petals from a daisy is an age-old tradition to discover whether your love is true. As you pluck the first petal, say "He (or she) loves me," then as you pluck each new petal, alternate between saying,

"*He loves me, he loves me not...*"

Do this until you have plucked all the petals from the flower. The last petal you pluck will give you your answer.

The Heart Line—Many believe that the lines of the palm reveal the possible paths of one's life. The line that crosses the top of your palm, directly below your fingers, is known as your Heart Line. This line is believed to reveal what fate holds for you regarding matters of love. The length of your Heart Line is said to indicate the length of your active love life. Lines that intersect your Heart Line represent conflicts or affairs that will interrupt your love life. Lines that branch outward from your main Heart Line represent the number of lovers you will have. The longer these branches are, the deeper the relationship they foretell. If the Heart Lines of your left hand and right hand are noticeably different, it means you will experience heartbreak before finding true love. If the lines are similar it means you will enjoy a healthy and well-balanced love life.

♥ *Searching for your Soul Mate*—Many people believe that destiny holds for them only one true love, one unique soul mate in all the world. To see what your true love looks like, hold a red candle in your right hand and stand facing a mirror in a darkened room. Slowly move the lit candle around your face while staring directly into the mirror and concentrate on finding your true love. After making six revolutions with the candle, blow out the flame and stare into the darkened mirror. The face of your true love will appear before your eyes.

♥ *Falling Apples*—To discover when you will meet your soulmate, pick up and remove all fallen apples beneath an apple tree and leave your apron spread out on the ground beneath the tree at night during a full moon. If an apple falls from the tree and lands on your apron, it is an omen that you have already met your true love. If no apples land on your apron, pick up the apple that has fallen the closest to it and cut it in half. If the apple has a worm inside, it means that your true love is currently involved with someone else. If the apple has no worms inside, count the number of seeds that are visible and remember this number. You will meet your soulmate before this same number of full moons pass.

AMULETS AND TALISMANS

The mystical arts have been wielded by mankind since long before the known sciences were discovered. Many practices utilize amulets and talismans that incorporate magical symbolism and sacred motifs to produce a specific desired effect.

Even in the modern day, it is not uncommon to adorn our bodies with charms and decorate our homes with wards to attain good luck, love, health or money, or to protect us from misfortune and fend off evil spirits.

THE TALISMAN OF VENUS

The Talisman of Venus is a powerful love charm. It is believed to bring good luck in affairs of the heart and ensure harmony in a relationship. It can be worn as a pendant close to one's heart, or inscribed on parchment and carried in one's pocket.

In centuries past, it was quite common for people to wear or carry magical charms or wards known as amulets to protect themselves from misfortune. These ornate charms were either inscribed with mystical symbols or empowered by a spell. Most amulets are worn as a pendant and are designed to offer protection against evil influences, injury or illness.

While the terms amulet and talisman are often used interchangeably, there is distinction between these two forms of charms. While both can be used as protective wards against misfortune and danger, only a talisman may also endow its owner with good luck, and in some cases, even grant the wearer enhanced abilities or mystical powers. Most talismans are designed for a specific purpose, and are custom-crafted for an individual person under favorable conditions, such as when certain planets are aligned. These types of talismans often consist of carved pieces of stone, metal, wood or bone that have been etched with mystical words or symbols. Simple talismans are often no more than pieces of parchment inscribed with sacred words, prayers or designs of symbolic significance. Mystics also utilized many natural talismans made from plants and animals.

ANIMAL CHARMS

BEZOAR—This stone-like calcium deposit found in the stomach of certain animals is believed to be an antidote for poison and a cure-all for many human afflictions.

CATS—The ancient Egyptians considered cats to be sacred creatures and believed that they possessed magical powers to protect against evil and to make wishes come true. A talisman fashioned in the likeness of a black cat is believed to ensure health and good luck.

BADGER—The tooth of a badger sewn inside a pocket is said to bring good fortune to gamblers.

BIRD'S EYE—During the Middle Ages, the eye of a rooster or other small bird worn in a bag around the neck was believed to protect the wearer from the influence of witchcraft and

also to bring good luck.

Scarab—The scarab beetle has been used in charms dating back as far as 5,000 years ago. The Egyptians regarded the scarab as a symbol of rebirth, the driving force which caused the sun to rise each day. They believed that placing the beetle in tombs would aid in the rebirth of the dead. Talismans fashioned in the form of a scarab were believed to bring good luck, health and strength.

Peacock—It is considered bad luck to display the feathers of this bird in a home. In past times, the eye-like markings on each feather were thought to resembling the "evil eye". However, an amulet containing an image of the bird itself is considered lucky and is thought to represent everlasting life.

Mole—The left hind foot of a mole, wrapped in silk, was once thought to be a ward against bad luck.

Rabbit's Foot—One of the most universal good luck charms is the rabbit's foot. Because of its ability to reproduce in such abundance, the rabbit was revered as an object of fertility and prosperity. It is believed that rubbing the belly of an expectant mother with a rabbit's foot will ensure a healthy birth. It was also once customary to brush a newborn baby with a rabbit's foot so that some of the charm's luck would rub off on the child. A rabbit's foot was also given as a gift to actors before their first performance to ensure fame and a long career. In the 1960's, rabbit's-foot key chains were a popular novelty item sold in stores across the country.

Spider—Considered by the ancient Etruscans to be a symbol of fortune, a spider talisman was thought to insure success in matters of business. During the Middle Ages, a live spider encased within two nutshell halves that have been bound together by silk was worn as a pendant to protect the wearer from illness.

PLANT TALISMANS

Mandrake—Because the root of the mandrake plant resembles the form of the human body, it is used as a key ingredient in many love spells. When placed under the bed it is considered to be a powerful charm for ensuring passion and fidelity.

Garlic—Besides its use as a repellent for vampires, its potency for warding off evil in all forms is held true by many cultures: Druids attributed magic virtues to it, and garlic cloves placed in each room of a dwelling were believed to ward off disease. In Poland, a clove of garlic is placed under the pillow of a sleeping child as protection, and Gypsies utilized garlic in many of their spells to ward off the "evil eye," and strings of garlic are often hung over doorways and windows to prevent evil spirits from entering a dwelling.

Lotus—The ancient Egyptians associated the lotus flower with the goddess Isis, for insight, wisdom, beauty and purity. In India, charms carved in the shape of the lotus blossom are worn for luck and good health. In Mesopotamia, the lotus was the flower of Lilith, the Sumero-Babylonian goddess, who according to Hebrew mythology, was the first woman, and Adam's original wife.

WORDS OF POWER

Groups of words believed to have mystical powers were often carved on temple walls and tombs to ward off evil spirits. Amulets of the same were also worn or sewn into clothing for personal protection from illness and accidents.

Abracadabra—This word is the most renowned and most ancient of magic words still used in the modern day. Its origin is thought to have derived from the Hebrew words *ha brachah dabarah*, which translates to "speak the blessing." In the form of an amulet, the word was inscribed on a piece of parchment, as follows, and worn around one's neck. This amulet is said to protect the wearer from disease, and was a popular charm during the Plague.

The Talisman of Angels—This is considered by some to be one of the most powerful of talismans. It contains the names of the angels who govern the seven planets. The angelic names and the planets they are associated with are as follows: Raphael (Sun); Zaphiel (Saturn); Zadkiel (Jupiter); Camael (Mars); Haniel (Venus); Michael (Mercury); Gabriel (Moon). The Latin verse *Invia virtuti nulla est via* translates to "There is no way impassable to virtue."

Word Squares—These talismans contain ancient words which can be read forwards, backwards, up and down. Such talismans can be written on parchment or inscribed in stone or wood. The top charm is used as a ward against evil spirits, and should be displayed at the threshold of your home. The bottom charm is an altered version which was designed to obtain true love and friendship. This talisman can be used as a seal on any letters that are sent to dear friends and loved ones, or carried in your pocket to attract the affections of others.

```
SATOR
AREPO
TENET
OPERA
ROTAS
```

```
SALOM
AREPO
LEMEL
OPERA
MOLAS
```

CROSSES

Long before the coming of Christianity, ancient people used the symbol of a cross in various forms as amulets and talismans.

The Tau Cross—Shaped like a letter T, this is one of the oldest of crosses. It symbolizes eternal life and is believed to protect the spirit of the wearer. The amulet also guards against disease and snake bites.

The Ankh—This symbol is a derivative of the Tau cross with the addition of a circle on top and was used by the ancient Egyptians to symbolize life and immortality. It was worn as an amulet and was emblazoned on many artifacts that represented their gods and goddesses.

The Cross of Saint Andrew—This cross is shaped like an X and is also considered a potent amulet against evil.

The Greek Cross—This cross, also called the Cross of Saint Benedict, is an equilateral cross carved into a medallion which is engraved with certain letters. It is said to protect the wearer from danger, both physical and spiritual. Each letter on the amulet represents Latin words:

The angles of the cross:
> CRUX SANCTI PATRIS
> BENEDICTI
> *(Cross of the Holy Father Benedict)*

The vertical bar:
> CRUX SANCTA SIT MIHI LUX
> *(O Holy Cross be my light)*

The horizontal bar:
> NE DAEMON SIT MIHI DUX
> *(Let no evil spirit be my guide)*

The letters around the circle:
> VADE RETRO SATANA
> *(Get thee behind me Satan)*
> NE SUADE MIHI VANA *(Suggest no vain delusions to me)*
> SUNT MALA QUAE LIBAS *(The things thou offerest are evil)*
> IPSE VENANA BIBAS *(Thou thyself drinkest poison)*

The Roman Cross—Though not originally a symbol of Christianity, this cross was bestowed with that special significance after the Crucifixion of Jesus, and in Christian cultures it is used more than any other religious talisman as a symbol of faith and a ward against evil.

SYMBOLIC TALISMANS

Hands—The ancient Egyptians regarded the hand as a symbol of fortitude. To the Romans, the hand represented loyalty and fidelity. The ancient Etruscans fashioned talismans in the form of the human hand as protection against the powers of witchcraft. In the Orient, a pendant in the form of a hand made from metal or blue-colored glass was used to protect against all forms of evil.

The Hand of Glory—This grisly talisman is fashioned from the hand of a hanged man. The severed hand is used as a macabre candelabra. It was believed that the light cast by the candle it held could reveal unseen things such as spirits or demons. The Hand of Glory was also used as a torch by thieves, for it was said that the candlelight could only be seen by the person who carried the hand.

The Hand of Benediction—This talisman is a life-sized carving of a hand kept in one's house as protection for those who live there as well as all their material possessions.

The Hand of Sabazius—Hands of this type are associated with the cult of the god Sabazius, which originated in Phrygia or Thrace and later became popular in the Roman Empire. Made of bronze, the hand features an odd array of symbolic representations including a serpent, cymbal, pine cone and frog. These talismans were placed in shrines or carried on poles in religious processions to ward off evil spirits.

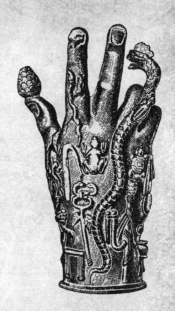

Mars & Venus—When these two planetary signs are intertwined, the resulting symbol represents the physical union of man and woman. A talisman depicting this symbol is usually worn to increase sexual potency, ensure fertility and bring strength to a relationship.

The Moon—Talismans in the shape of the crescent moon were worn by women of ancient Rome in order to ensure fertility, and also as protection against illness and evil spirits.

Keys—This item was often worn as a talisman by the ancient Greeks who considered the key to be a symbol of the two-headed god Janus, the guardian of all doors. Because Janus had the ability to see into the future, this talisman was believed to bestow the wearer with the gift of foresight and good judgment.

Hearts—The heart was originally believed to the resting place of the soul and all human affections. Amulets fashioned in the form of a heart are often given as a promise of true love and are believed to ensure fidelity in a relationship. This charm is especially effective when made form a red stone such as a ruby, carnelian or garnet.

The Eye of Horus—To the ancient Egyptians, this charm, referred to as the *Udjat*, represented the process of 'making whole' and healing. They believed that the eyes of the god Horus were in fact the Sun and the Moon, the left eye representing the moon, the right the sun. The Udjat was used on emblems to signify monarchy or kingship. As an amulet it was reputed for its great healing and protective powers, and was implemented during funeral rites, being placed on or inside a mummy, to protect the soul of the dead. A particularly strong talisman would incorporate both the left and right eyes.

Gems

Whether worn as a pendant or fashioned into a necklace, certain gems, minerals or stones are believed to bestow good fortune and protect the wearer from evil influences.

Amber—In some cultures, beads made of amber are thought to bring good fortune to a bride on her wedding day, ensuring fidelity and fertility. In Italy, amber necklaces are worn as protection against ailments of the throat, and in some areas of Russia they are thought to bring long life to the wearer.

Bloodstone—This dark green stone is flecked with bits of red and is used to ensure victory in battle. When worn on a pendant against the chest, it is said to aid in the healing of wounds. It is also believed that the bloodstone has the power to create lightning storms, and that it bestows the power of prophecy upon the wearer.

Cat's Eye—This stone is usually gray, green or brown, with striations that look like the eye of a cat. The most highly valued is the green variety. It is often used as protection against the dreaded "evil eye". The Cat's Eye also has healing properties and is thought to open the heart to goodness and charitable deeds.

Coral—Beads made of red coral are considered healthy, are said to stop internal bleeding, and are used to ward off misfortune or accidents. The ancient Romans fashioned collars from coral and flint for their pets to prevent hydrophobia.

Garnets—These gems come in a variety of colors (various shades of red, pink, orange, purple or green) with burgundy being the most common. In the Middle Ages, garnets were used to drive away demons and nightmares, and to increase chivalry, loyalty and honesty. The red variety is said to promote passion in all areas of life.

Jet—This is a compact mineral, with a velvety appearance like coal, derived from petrified trees. Beads made of jet are said to inspire hope and fortitude in the wearer, and was used as a protection against snakebite or scorpion stings.

Onyx—Eye beads made from onyx represent the all-seeing deity, and as such they protect the wearer from danger. Onyx beads are considered particularly lucky, especially for women in matters of love. If engraved with the likeness of a camel's head, the wearer will suffer nightmares.

Sapphire—Generally, any bead made of blue glass or stone has long been thought to ensure chastity or faithfulness in a lover. A sapphire carved with the likeness of a ram was used by the ancients to cure eye diseases.

The Mystical Properties of Birthstones

For countless centuries mankind has cherished rare and beautiful gemstones, with the belief that they possess magical properties. Some stones were believed to bring good luck while others were thought to have healing powers. Such attributes were usually based on the stone's color or the region in which the gem was mined and differed from culture to culture.

The mystical associations of gemstones have varied throughout the ages, but one concept that many scholars attest to is derived from ancient scripture. It was written that the high priest Aaron had worn a breastplate adorned with twelve gems representative of the twelve tribes of Israel. Eventually, astrologers transferred the religious symbolism of certain gems to the twelve signs of the Zodiac. Because the calendar has been revised over time and the modern months no longer correspond exactly with the signs of the Zodiac, the idea evolved to encompass the calendar month of one's birth.

The idea of a "birthstone" became popularized during the 18th century, but the stones associated with each month continued to change until 1912, when the National Association of Jewelers decided to standardize the list of birthstones and assign specific gems to each month. The following list shows the birthstones as they are widely recognized today, as well as the mystical properties associated with each of the gemstones. Amulets fashioned from such are typically chosen for their mystical properties or as a representation of a personality trait, and are bestowed according to the birth date of the wearer. Some are worn for health and luck, while others are believed to be wards against evil. In some cases, even the setting of a particular gem is of importance, and some are believed to be unlucky for anyone to wear except for those who can rightfully claim it as their own.

JANUARY ✦ GARNET

Color: *dark red*
Zodiac: *Capricorn (Dec. 22–Jan. 19)*
Garnet is a symbol of health, consistency, and perseverance. Garnets are said to enhance memory and prevent depression. In ancient Egyptian culture, garnets signified passion, loyalty, and long-lasting love. The French call this stone *gouette de sange,* which means "drop of blood." According to biblical legend, Noah suspended a garnet in the Ark to disperse light, hence, the garnet is sometimes called "Noah's Lantern."

Garnets were used during the Middle Ages to provide guidance during night travel and worn as a protection from nightmares. Slivers of this red gem were once used in stained glass windows in medieval cathedrals. Garnets were also used in charms to protect against thieves—'tis said a stolen garnet will bring bad luck until returned to its rightful owner.

FEBRUARY ✦ AMETHYST

Color: *light violet to dark purple*
Zodiac: *Aquarius (Jan. 20–Feb. 18)*
Amethyst is a symbol of sincerity, security, and peace of mind. Amethyst is thought to be a meditative aid, and can be placed under one's pillow as a charm against insomnia. This gem enhances psychic powers as well, and is sometimes kept with tarot cards or other divination tools. In the early Renaissance, it was believed to prevent evil thoughts. The ancient Greeks and Romans proclaimed that wearing amethyst would prevent intoxication. Amethyst was said to have been created by Bacchus, the Roman god of wine. When a beautiful young maiden cried out to the goddess Diana for protection against the murderous wrath of Bacchus, Diana encased the woman inside a beautiful clear crystal. Bacchus, regretting his violent act, anointed the girl with wine and brought her back to life, thus changing the clear crystal to purple. Even today some claim that amethyst helps achieve sobriety and use it to aid in recovery from addiction.

MARCH ◂ AQUAMARINE

Color: pale blue-green
Zodiac: Pisces (Feb. 19–Mar. 20)
Aquamarine is a symbol of calmness, safety and serenity. Healing properties associated with this gem include help with digestive troubles. According to legend, aquamarine was created by the great sea monster Leviathan, the weight of its body compressing the seawater into stone. Aquamarine is also a favorite gem of sea goddesses and sirens. Because of its association with the sea, aquamarine was a favorite luck charm among ancient mariners.

APRIL ◂ DIAMOND

Color: clear
Zodiac: Aries (Mar. 21–Apr. 20)
Diamond represents innocence, honesty and purity, hence, its popularity as a wedding jewel. Diamonds are said to increase mental clarity as well as intensify the qualities of the wearer, whatever those qualities might be. Diamonds are said to remove evil thoughts, yet it seems these rare gems also inspire greed due to the fact they are so extremely expensive. Referred to as the "king gem," the diamond was used during the Middle Ages as an emblem of fearlessness and invincibility.

MAY ◂ EMERALD

Color: deep, vibrant green
Zodiac: Taurus (Apr. 21–May 20)
Emeralds are associated with health, love and success. Hindu healers of India used this stone as a curative for various stomach-related illnesses. They inscribed them with sacred text and wore them as talismans, believing the emerald had the power to drive away demons and rid the body of evil spirits. According to other legends, emeralds assisted in predicting the future and were thought to aid in preventing vision loss. Ancient Egyptians believed that the stone would repel venomous snakes and protect against poisons. It was said to be the stone of the goddess Isis, and that anyone who gazed upon her jewel would be assured a safe voyage to the Underworld. In Greek mythology, the emerald was associated with Aphrodite, the goddess of love and beauty. Emeralds are also associated with mental clarity and perception.

JUNE ◂ PEARL

Color: white or light gray
with a multicolor sheen
Zodiac: Gemini (May 21–June 21)
Pearls symbolize love, longevity and happiness. Pearls were once thought by Arabs to be the "tears of gods," formed when raindrops fell into oyster shells. Pearl is often referred to as the "queen gem," and was used during the Middle Ages as an emblem of modesty, chastity and purity. Powdered pearl mixed with sap from an ash tree was also believed to be a remedy for the plague. Pearl was mixed in various concoctions and used as a healing potion for everything from headaches to leprosy. In more recent centuries, it was employed as an aphrodisiac and

was also ground up as an additive in toothpaste. In the Victorian Era, pearls were considered appropriate jewelry for young, unmarried women, as a symbol of purity. They were gifted to married women by their husbands to symbolize fidelity. In India, the pearl symbolizes a happy marriage and is given as a wedding gift.

JULY ✦ RUBY
Color: deep, vivid red
Zodiac: Cancer (June 22–July 22)
Rubies represent freedom and contentment, as well as glory, power and passion. The stone is said to open one's heart to love, and some ancient lore holds that a ruby is capable of reconciling a lovers' quarrel. They were once widely believed to ensure safety from peril, and to ward off misfortune and ill health. Because of their color, medieval physicians believed rubies were good for the blood. The ancient Chinese engraved rubies with depictions of dragons and snakes, believing the charms would bring wealth and power. In Myanmar (formerly Burma), where most of the world's rubies are mined, it was common practice for warriors to insert a ruby beneath their skin as a ward of protection before entering into battle.

AUGUST ✦ PERIDOT
Color: pale green
Zodiac: Leo (July 23–August 22)
Peridot symbolizes fame, dignity, friendship and marital bliss. This gem is also valued for its healing properties. It has been employed in mystical rites for channeling visions, and used as a charm to soothe anger, jealousy and envy. The powers of peridot are said to be doubled when set in gold. For 3500 years, peridot was mined from a small island off the coast of Egypt. It was said that Cleopatra, queen of the Nile, adorned herself with peridot because, like emerald, it provided protection from venomous serpents. Peridot was also believed to provide protection against evil. During the Crusades, the Templar Knights brought this stone back with them, which was used to adorn holy relics and cathedral windows.

SEPTEMBER ✦ SAPPHIRE
Color: light to dark blue
Zodiac: Virgo (Aug. 23–Sept. 22)
Sapphire is associated with hope, joy, truth, sincerity, and mental clarity. The Egyptians used blue sapphire to designate the Eye of Horus, and the stone has since been prized as a curative for eye problems. In the Middle Ages, sapphires were believed to promote tranquility and peace of mind, and to suppress wicked and impure thoughts. The stone was said to protect the wearer against envy and attract divine favor. Royalty wore sapphires as a powerful ward against harm, especially poison. In Buddhist culture, sapphires symbolized devotion and enlightenment. The Greeks associated sapphire with the god Apollo, and, believing the stone

to be an aid to prophecy, used it when consulting the Oracles at Delphi. Sapphire is also said to aid in the fulfillment of dreams.

OCTOBER — OPAL

Color: black, dark blue or white with fiery bursts of color
Zodiac: Libra (Sept. 23–Oct. 22)

Opal is a symbol of hope, faithfulness, confidence and truth. Arabs believed that opals fell from heaven during lightning storms, thus explaining the stone's otherworldly color display. It was once believed that opals had the power to render a person invisible, and for this reason they were considered lucky for thieves. Some claim that opals are very unlucky for anyone else but those who can claim it as their birthstone. Folklore holds that opals act like a "mood ring," bright when the wearer is well and in good spirits, turning cloudy when the wearer is ill or near death. In the Middle Ages, opal was called *ophthalmios,* meaning "eye stone," due to a widespread belief that it offered a cure for eye disorders. Other reputed healing properties include prevention from infection and a cure for weakness of the heart. It is used to increase mental capacities and untapped powers of the mind. Black opals are considered the tools of choice for witches and magicians, who use them primarily to enhance their receptive or projective powers. Black opals are also said to ward off evil and protect travelers.

NOVEMBER — TOPAZ

Color: golden yellow
Zodiac: Scorpio (Oct. 23–Nov. 21)

Topaz symbolizes loyalty, wisdom, creativity and mental power. It is a traditional stone for writers, scholars, and artists. The ancient Greeks associated topaz with strength and courage. The figure of a falcon carved on topaz was thought to help acquire the goodwill of kings. Set in gold and worn as a bracelet on the left arm, it was considered a ward against evil magic. Powdered and mixed with wine, it was once thought to cure insanity and diseases of the eye. Medieval physicians also employed topaz as a cure for the plague.

DECEMBER — TURQUOISE

Color: blue-green
Zodiac: Sagittarius (Nov. 22–Dec. 21)

Turquoise represents success, self-motivation and prosperity. The virtuous properties of turquoise are said to exist only if the stone is given as a gift. Turquoise has been thought to warn the wearer of danger or illness by changing its shade of color. It was thought to protect the wearer from falling, especially from horses. Medieval Turks would attach turquoise to the bridles of their horses as an amulet of protection for the animals. Indians believed that if turquoise was affixed to a bow, the arrows shot from it would always aim true.

THE ART OF PENDULUM DIVINATION

The art of Pendulum dowsing is perhaps one of the oldest known methods of divination.

The following pages offer a brief history of this prophetic tool, how to make one, and its many uses from answering everyday questions, to reading the past, present and future, divining the truth, and even finding lost treasure.

♈	ARIES —THE RAM March 21 to April 20	
♉	TAURUS — THE BULL April 21 to May 20	
♊	GEMINI — THE TWINS May 21 to June 21	
♋	CANCER — THE CRAB June 22 to July 22	
♌	LEO — THE LION July 23 to August 22	
♍	VIRGO — THE VIRGIN August 23 to September 22	

♎	LIBRA — THE SCALES September 23 to October 22	
♏	SCORPIO — THE SCORPION October 23 to November 21	
♐	SAGITTARIUS — THE ARCHER November 22 to December 21	
♑	CAPRICORN — THE GOAT December 22 to January 19	
♒	AQUARIUS — WATER BEARER January 20 to February 18	
♓	PISCES — THE FISH February 19 to March 20	

 AIR

 FIRE

 EARTH

 WATER

HISTORY OF PENDULUM DIVINATION

Pendulum divination has survived for well over a thousand years. As early as 300 A.D. the pendulum was used as a scrying tool by the ancient Romans to foretell who would succeed the Emperor and to determine the outcome of impending battles. The infamous French seer Nostradamus was renowned for his use of the pendulum to predict future events.

The ancient mystics employed the pendulum method of basin scrying in which a bowl made of electrum, an alloy of gold and silver, was engraved or painted with the twenty-four letters of the Greek alphabet. A ring, engraved with occult characters, was attached by thread to a wand made from a laurel branch. After a question was posed by the scryer, the pendulum would begin to swing. When its momentum gathered, the ring would hit at different points inside the rim of the basin where the alphabet was carved. Each time the ring hit a letter, it spelled out words to a prophetic verse.

HOW TO MAKE A PENDULUM

A pendulum consists of any weighted object which hangs freely from a chain or string. Pendulums can be made of anything—a pendant necklace, a quartz crystal attached to a single length of silver chain, or a ring suspended from a silk thread. Whatever the item, it should be heavy enough for the string or chain to hang straight and taut. The best type of pendulum is one made from items having some personal meaning to you.

For the best results, a handle should be attached to the upper end of the chain or string to allow the weight to swing freely. A bead, a small charm, or a short wand will do.

Cleansing & Purification

Whether you have purchased your pendulum from a store, received it as a gift, or made it by hand, it should be cleansed to remove any past residue of outside energies. There are many methods of purification such as holding the pendulum under cold, running water, dipping it in sea salt, or smudging it with the ashes from burnt incense, or by leaving the pendulum to bask in the light of a full moon overnight.

Bonding Energies

For the most accurate results, allow your pendulum to become attuned to your energy. Carry it with you for a few days, keeping it close to your heart on a necklace, or wrap it in a velvet or silk cloth and keep it on your person.

How To Use A Pendulum

Begin by first choosing a table and chair that provide a comfortable height for working. Sit with your elbow on the table. Using the hand you do *not* use for writing, hold the handle loosely between your thumb and forefinger, bending your wrist to allow the pendulum to hang straight down. The pendulum should be positioned approximately ½ to 1 inch above the center of the oracle diagram. Relax, making sure your hand and arm are completely still. Wait until the pendulum has stopped swinging before you pose a question.

Ask A Question—You may begin asking your questions, keeping in mind that each inquiry must be phrased as a "Yes" or "No" question. Ask your question out loud, and focus your mind on it until the pendulum begins to sway. If the pendulum swings in an *up-and-down* direction, the answer to your question is "Yes." If the pendulum swings in a *side-to-side* direction, the answer is "No." If the pendulum moves in a *circular* motion, read the response as such: *Clockwise* for "Yes." *Counter-clockwise* for "No." It is important to stop and center the pendulum between each question so that the momentum will not influence the next response. Be prepared to ask several questions to gather enough information to aid you in your quest. As your skill increases, you will discover how to pose a question to avoid any erratic behavior which may result in vague responses.

Advanced Methods

Once you have mastered the basic yes/no method, you may want to try using your pendulum to aid you with more complex questions.

Using The Oracle Diagram on the first page will allow you to ascertain more information with your pendulum. The astrological symbols around the diagram represent the twelve signs of the Western Zodiac. If your pendulum guides you to one or more of these symbols, use the symbol key below the diagram to find the matching sun sign which represents someone who may influence the outcome of your quest. The elemental symbols represent the forces of nature that you will encounter on your quest.

AIR — The unseen forces of nature, representing the spiritual and ethereal, and those who are lighthearted and free.

EARTH — The passive forces of nature, representing logic, reason and those who are grounded and dependable.

FIRE — The destructive forces of nature, representing conflict, disruption, and those who are passionate and temperamental.

WATER — The nurturing forces of nature, representing intuition, growth and those who are caring and persistent.

Basin Scrying

Like the ancient mystics, you may use the letters on the diagram to spell out words or sentences to questions that cannot be answered with a simple yes or no response. Begin at the center of the diagram, allowing the pendulum to still itself, pose your question, then watch where the pendulum swings. Record each letter that the pendulum swings towards, then decipher the prophecy. It may help to have a friend write down the letters for you. You will know the verse is complete when your pendulum loses its momentum or the final letter falls into place. If your pendulum begins to swing in a circular motion during a scrying session, it is designating a time frame. A *clockwise* motion foretells that the message will unfold in the future. If your pendulum spins in a *counter-clockwise* direction, then the message will pertain to past events.

You may choose to make your own scrying basin out of clay, or simply paint the alphabet inside the rim of an existing bowl, decorating it how you see fit. The bowl should have a wide mouth, about 8 inches in diameter, with a shallow base.

Goblet Scrying

Fill a goblet or heavy glass with water, about three-quarters full. Hold your pendulum so that it is positioned in the exact center and slightly inside the rim of the cup, but do not allow it to touch the water. Wait for the pendulum to still itself, then pose your question. After time, the pendulum should begin to swing and hit the rim of the goblet. A *single tap* indicates "Yes," while *two taps* indicates "No." *More than two taps* indicates uncertainty—ask again later.

Other Uses

Whatever you seek, whatever question you have, the pendulum can be your guide. *Ghost Hunting*—To determine whether or not a ghost or spirit is present in a particular location, suspend your pendulum from a stable object such as a chair or lamp near the center of the room, making sure that it is free of any drafts. If the pendulum begins to sway it designates a spiritual presence.

LIE DETECTOR—To determine whether or not someone is telling you the truth, hold your pendulum over their right palm and ask them a question. After they answer, your pendulum will reveal if they are being honest. If the pendulum begins to swing in a *straight line,* it designates that they are telling the truth. If the pendulum swings in a *circular motion* it means that they are being deceptive.

DOWSING FOR WATER—The pendulum may also be used like a dowsing rod. Walk through an area while holding the pendulum in front of you. If it begins to spin, you will likely find water underfoot.

DETERMINING GENDER—The pendulum can be used to predict the sex of unborn children. Hold the pendulum over the right palm of a mother-to-be. If the pendulum swings back and forth in a *straight line,* then the mother will deliver a boy. If the pendulum swings in a *circular motion,* the child will be a girl.

FINDING LOST ITEMS —The pendulum is employed in this way by holding it over a map of the area where you think you may have lost what you are searching for. The "map" may also be a simple diagram of your house which you have drawn for this purpose. Slowly move the pendulum over each section on the map until it spins or moves in small circles. This should indicate the area where the lost item is to be found.

HOW THE PENDULUM WORKS

The theory by which the pendulum functions is based on two factors: that which is embedded or hidden within the subconscious mind and the electro-magnetic energy field that surrounds all living things.

The subconscious mind holds the key to unlocking many mysteries. This part of the mind is sometimes referred to as one's "Higher Self." It holds the answers to the past, present and future, and can provide spiritual solutions to some of life's dilemmas.

The pendulum works as a vehicle for moving information from the subconscious to the conscious mind to bring us the answers we seek.

Sometimes the solutions to the most difficult problems are simple. Accept the responses you may get only if your instincts agree that it is the best path to follow and that harm will come to none.

CANDLE MAGIC

Ever since the discovery of fire
by our earliest ancestors,
people have gazed deep into
the flickering flames to discern
its magical properties. As one
of the four elemental powers,
fire has long been seen as a
destructive force, however,
many believe that it can also
be used as a portal to the
spirit realm. The ancient
Druids looked to the burnt
remains of their sacrifices for
signs from their gods. Since
those primitive times, the
mystical art of using candles to
divine future events has been
widely practiced for centuries.

CHOOSING A COLOR

Color is very important in candle magic when trying to achieve a particular goal. Each color is connected with the astrological signs of the Zodiac and their planetary rulers. In some cases, a particular shade of color may help to further influence one's ritual. For example, Venus is typically associated with the colors green and pink. The signs under the rule of Mercury are represented with yellow, but pale green or pale blue have also been used. The Moon can be silver or white, the Sun is typically gold or golden yellow, and Mars can range from orange to bright red to reddish-brown. Pisces can be blue or green or a shade in between such as aqua. Uranus is typically represented by all colors, as in a rainbow spectrum, but white may suffice as a neutral non-color. The standard colors used in candle magic and their influences are:

White—represents purity, spirituality and peace. White may also be used as a stand-in for any other color.

Red—associated with the element of Fire, represents energy, strength, passion, lust, and courage.

Pink—used in matters of love, affection and friendship.

Orange—used for financial gain, career advancement, or matters of a legal nature.

Yellow—associated with the element of Air, represents intellect and imagination, used to promote memory, communication and higher learning.

Green—associated with the element of Earth, represents abundance, fertility and prosperity, used primarily to promote health and healing and for solving financial problems.

Blue—associated with the element of Water, represents truth, wisdom and loyalty, has calming properties, brings about inspiration and facilitates communication.

Purple—used during spiritual meditation to enhance psychic ability, has the power to influence others.

Gold—represents masculine power, ambition and justice.

Silver—represents feminine power, promotes clairvoyance, dreams and intuition.

Black—for binding spells or banishing negative energy.

DRESSING THE CANDLE

Herbs, incense and essential oils are often used to add extra symbolism to a ritual. This process is referred to as "dressing" the candle. The candle may be coated with fragrant oil (just a couple drops is enough for a 3" pillar candle) or lightly dusted with powdered herbs or incense before lighting. However, do take care while burning to make sure the ingredients don't spark and set off a blaze. You may also carve names, runes or some other symbol into the wax before dressing the candle. Following is a brief list of easily attainable herbs, oils and floral scents. The powdered or oil forms are interchangeable:

Almond—for prosperity, wisdom and to guide divination.

Anise—to prevent nightmares and enhance prophetic dreams, and to promote romance and happiness.

Basil—for love, fidelity, strength and tranquility.

Bayberry—for good luck, peace, harmony and well-being, a ward against violence.

Catnip—for strength, courage, love, beauty and happiness.

Cedar—to cleanse and purify or to attract prosperity.

Cherry—for love and good luck in beginning a new endeavor.

Cinnamon—to promote passion, energy and business success.

Citronella (Lemongrass)—promotes creativity and mental clarity, brings prosperity, and used as insect repellent.

Clove—for purification and protection from enemies, promotes love and friendship.

Eucalyptus—to promote health or protect from illness.

Ginseng—to break curses and hexes.

Honeysuckle—to increase psychic powers of divination.

Jasmine—for luck and wealth, an aid to bring about prophetic dreams, also an aphrodisiac.

Lavender—for relaxation, healing, fidelity, aids the granting of a wish.

Sage—for long life, wisdom, healing, protection and banishing.

Sandalwood—for purification, protection, meditation, healing, sexual attraction and granting wishes.

Mint (all kinds)—for restoring energy, granting wishes, healing, love, money and protection during travel.

Mulberry—for physical and emotional strength.

Myrrh—an aid for meditation, to promote energy and healing, to protect from hexes and curses.

Orange Blossom—for love, beauty and good luck.

Passion Flower—to promote friendship and understanding, an aid for personal betterment, also a sleeping aid.

Patchouli—an aphrodisiac, promotes lust, attracts money, a divinatory aid.

Rose/Rosemary—for love, confidence, healing, also provides a calming effect and aids sleep.

Sesame—for money or lust.

Strawberry—for luck and love.

Vanilla—promotes love, lust and aids mental awareness.

Candle Prophecy

This requires a candle or oil lamp with a wick, for it is the behavior of the flame and wick that will provide the omen. The ancient Egyptians employed this method of fortune-telling using a single candle—the reading of which was done only by a child, as it was believed that children were closer to the gods and more open to purer perceptions. The Greeks devised a method using four candles; three candles were placed in a triangular shape with a fourth placed in the center. It was believed that the three outer candles attracted spirits, who revealed their messages via the central flame, which would in turn provide the prophecy.

To begin, ask a question, either voicing it aloud or considering it silently, then interpret the behavior of the flame and wick. Following are some interpretations:

A *small but bright flame* answers "Yes" to the query. A flame that slowly dies or extinguishes itself immediately indicates a definitive "No" to the question. If the flame suddenly goes out after burning brightly for some time, this is a bad omen indicating that disaster may follow.

A *large, steady bright flame* and a glowing wick promises great success and urges you to continue on your present path. If the flame burns dimly yet does not actually go out, there will very likely be a setback and it may take a while longer to achieve your goal.

If *the flame or wick leans to one side*, a significant change is coming, either in one's own circumstance or in a relationship. This might also indicate a journey that one must endeavor to make alone.

A *flickering flame* indicates a more sudden change, possibly in finances or career. A sparkling flame indicates a concern about health or safety, and caution should be taken. If the flame twists and burns high, beware of outside opposition or of someone attempting to thwart your plans.

INCORPORATING THE ZODIAC

If you are conducting a magical ritual which involves a person who cannot be present, they can be symbolically represented by another colored candle. You need to know the person's birth date and burn the appropriate color for that Zodiac sign. The colors correspond to the ruling planet of each sign and take into consideration other factors such as the elements most closely linked to the sign.

Zodiac Sign	Ruling Planet	Color
Aquarius (Jan 20-Feb 18)	Uranus	White
Pisces (Feb 19-Mar 20)	Neptune	Blue
Aries (March 21–April 20)	Mars	Red
Taurus (April 21–May 20)	Venus	Green
Gemini (May 21–June 21)	Mercury	Yellow
Cancer (June 22–July 22)	Moon	Silver
Leo (July 23–Aug 22)	Sun	Gold
Virgo (Aug 23–Sept 22)	Mercury	Yellow
Libra (Sept 23–Oct 22)	Venus	Pink
Scorpio (Oct 23–Nov 21)	Mars	Orange
Sagittarius (Nov 23–Dec 21)	Jupiter	Purple
Capricorn (Dec 22–Jan 19)	Saturn	Black

MAKING A WISH

First, choose the color of candle that best represents the type of goal you are attempting to achieve. It is recommended that you use a new candle that has not yet been used for any other purpose. It is also a good idea to conduct this ritual on a non-flammable surface that's easily cleaned up, such as a large cookie sheet covered in tin foil. A pair of tweezers will also come in handy.

Write down what you want to accomplish on a clean piece of paper. You may use colored paper that matches the candle if you choose. When you have completed your petition, fold up the paper three times crosswise. Using tweezers, hold the edge of the folded paper to the candle flame and allow it to burn completely to ash.

As it burns, visualize your circumstances and imagine your dream coming true. Gather the ashes, making sure they are completely out, crush them and toss them outdoors into the breeze to carry your wish upon the wind.

CEROMANCY

This technique uses melted wax as a means to divine the future. A natural candle (as opposed to a "dripless" candle) works best for this. Any color may be used. You will also need a bowl of very cold water. Ask your question or concentrate on the situation while allowing the candle to burn until a fair amount of hot wax forms. Then let the wax drip into the bowl of cold water. The various shapes created from the cooling bits of wax are thus interpreted:

APPLE—creativity, accomplishment, productivity and success.

ANT—hard work and an industrious attitude is required; indicates a period of fast progress.

ANCHOR—stability is assured yet this also warns against becoming too stagnant or complacent.

ARROW—an important message.

AX—a threat of possible trouble ahead.

BELL—an unexpected announcement.

BIRD—good news is on the way.

BUTTERFLY—happiness, innocence, the pleasures of friendship.

CAT—beware a betrayal, an untrue friend.

CLAW—an unknown enemy.

CLOVER—good luck.

CROWN—indicates qualities of leadership; a time to take charge of the situation.

DAGGER/SWORD—a dangerous undertaking or someone plotting against you, a relationship may be severed, an indication of family strife.

DIAMOND—an encouragement to reach higher, but take care that your ideal is not so lofty that it's impossible to reach your goal.

DOTS—money, more dots indicate more money to come.

EGG—success in future plans

FISH—material gain, spiritual growth.

FLOWER—friendship, praise from contemporaries, a tribute.

FOOT—leave the past behind, move forward.

HAND—accept help if it is offered.

HANGMAN'S NOOSE—a warning to proceed with caution in business matters.

HEART—care and love.

HOOK—an eagerness for knowledge, the sharing of wisdom.

HORSESHOE—very fortunate.

INSECT—small problems that will irritate but can be overcome.

KNOT—a complex problem.

LADDER—an opportunity for promotion, hard work ahead.

LEAF—good health.

MOON/CRESCENT—a change in one's situation.

MUSICAL NOTE—a harmonious partnership or venture.

RABBIT—a fun-loving friend will arrive to lift your spirits.

RAT/MOUSE—beware of dishonesty or theft.

RING—a proposal of marriage, a happy union, fidelity, a change for the better, completion.

SNAKE—a journey, an adventure or a concern about what lies ahead.

SPIRAL—progress is slow, patience is required, treachery may lie ahead.

SPOON—plenty of things are happening right now, take each one at a time or you may be overwhelmed.

SQUARE—stubbornness, complacency, an unwillingness to see things from a different perspective.

STAR—a very fortunate sign, a successful project, recognition for your hard work.

TREE—a time of personal growth and success.

TRIANGLE/PYRAMID—an omen of success and personal achievement.

TRIDENT—a decision must be made.

UMBRELLA—protection, someone is concerned with your well-being and is looking out for you.

WORMS—beware of scandal and embarrassment.

LABYRINTHS, MAZES AND CELTIC KNOTS

From the cavernous lair of the Minotaur of ancient Crete to the artistic designs of Medieval cathedrals, labyrinths and mazes have cast an air of mystique for countless centuries. Primarily used for meditation and prayer, the labyrinthine designs of old have developed into a form of art that can be seen in everything from Celtic knotwork patterns to the garden mazes of the Renaissance period.

THE LABYRINTH OF ANCIENT CRETE

The Labyrinth of ancient Crete was the lair of a monster known as the Minotaur, a mythical beast with the body of a man and the head of a bull. During the reign of King Minos, young men and maidens were cast into the cavernous maze of tunnels to serve as human sacrifices to the Minotaur. All of the victims who became lost in the maze were devoured by the beast until the hero, Theseus, killed the Minotaur and found his way back out by following a trail of twine that he had left to mark his path.

ANCIENT HISTORY

A labyrinth is considered by most scholars to be a single circuitous path with only one entrance that leads through a series of switchbacks to its center, then out again. The intention is that one will always find his or her way, and that there is no right or wrong way. A maze, by contrast, will invariably lead to dead-ends and blind alleys with the intention of causing confusion and mystery. The two words, however, are often used interchangeably.

Labyrinth designs found on ancient Cretan coins.

Over the years historians have categorized labyrinths into two basic patterns. The Cretan style (also called the Seven-circuit or Classic), which is the oldest known design, was found on coins from Crete and in renderings of Greek scholars, and was therefore associated with the Minotaur of legend. Variations on this Classic design also appear in Celtic culture as seen in their famously intricate knotwork, and on pottery and woven materials from the Americas. The design utilizes spiral forms, symbolizing life's journey.

The Chartres style, named for the design on the floor of the medieval Cathedral of Notre Dame in Chartres, France, is a mathematical marvel containing eleven circuits, turning thirty-four times with alternating lefts and rights, each turn being exactly 1/2 or 1/4 of the circumference. This quartering pattern is indicative of designs from the Middle Ages. Many of the medieval labyrinths surviving today can be found in cathedrals across France.

Labyrinths have been used as a spiritual tool for over four thousand years. Examples can be found on almost every inhabited continent in the world. Some of the most elaborate designs can still be seen in cathedrals throughout Europe, on pottery, weavings and artwork from Greece, Egypt, India, Peru and the American Southwest.

The "Man in the Maze," a popular Native American maze design.

A triple spiral, indicative of Celtic labyrinth designs.

"Shepard's Race," common to Ireland, Scotland and Wales.

A massive labyrinth of Egyptian design was reportedly built around 2300 BC by King Amenemhat III. According to written accounts, the temple which marked the labyrinth measured 165 by 80 feet and stood two stories tall. The labyrinth was believed to extend to a network of underground tunnels, covering a much broader area.

The most famous labyrinth of all, attributed to Greek mythology, is believed to have existed in an actual archeological location, in the city of Knossos on the isle of Crete. The city and palace have since been excavated but no labyrinth was ever found. According to legend, King Minos ordered a massive underground labyrinth to be built beneath the palace at Knossos to imprison the Minotaur, a monstrous creature with the head and tail of a bull and the body of a man that was the unfortunate result of a union between Minos' wife Pasiphae and a prized bull given to him by the god Poseidon, whom Minos had angered. As the story goes, Minos had asked for Poseidon's blessing in making him king. Poseidon sent Minos the white bull as a sign of favor with the agreement that Minos would then sacrifice the bull back to Poseidon upon achieving the throne. But Minos kept the bull for himself. So, Poseidon made Pasiphae fall in love with the bull.

Later, when Minos' son was murdered, the king declared war on the city of Athens, demanding sacrifice as tribute. Each year, Athenian boys and maidens were sent to Crete to be locked in the labyrinth for the Minotaur to feast upon. When a young hero by the name of Theseus learned of the sacrifices, he went to Crete to challenge the beast. Upon his arrival, he met the king's daughter, princess Ariadne, and the two fell in love. On the day that Theseus was thrown into the labyrinth, Ariadne provided him with a simple ball of twine, which he was to fasten close to the entrance of the maze, unwinding it as he made his way through the dark, winding passages. When Theseus encountered the Minotaur, he killed the beast, then followed the thread to make his escape.

A stone labyrinth found in Ravenna, Italy.

THE MEDIEVAL LABYRINTH

During the Middle Ages, cathedrals were designed with labyrinths fashioned into the tiles of the floor. Patrons would enter at one end and slowly walk the winding path while meditating, praying and contemplating upon their lives in search of enlightenment. Those who continue this age-old practice find that every labyrinth has a different rhythm and that walking the pattern slows breathing, calms and focuses the mind, and brings about an overall state of personal tranquility.

A ceiling tile from the Gonzaga palace of Mantua, Italy. The Gonzaga family motto inscribed along the path reads "maybe yes, maybe no."

Notre-Dame de Chartres

Amiens Cathedral, France

Saint Omer Church, France

Reims Cathedral, France

GARDEN MAZES

From the late 17th century through the early 19th century, topiary artists sculpted living hedges into magnificent garden mazes, and labyrinths underwent a transformation to become an extravagant form of entertainment.

The garden maze at Hampton Court Palace near London is the United Kingdom's oldest surviving hedge maze. It was commissioned in 1690 by King William III after he arrived in England with his wife Queen Mary to take over the English throne. Its unusual trapezoid shape covers a third of an acre and its paths measure one-half of a mile.

The Longleat House in Wiltshire, England boasts a collection of contemporary mazes including a giant hedge maze. The Longleat Hedge Maze covers an area of 1.48 acres with a pathway measuring 1.69 miles. Six wooden bridges offer glimpses towards the center of the maze, which is marked by an observation tower. Longleat also has a rose garden maze called the "Labyrinth of Love," which provides a backdrop for wedding ceremonies held on the manor grounds. It also has a "Sun Maze," and a "Lunar Labyrinth" in addition to "King Arthur's Mirror Maze."

CELTIC KNOTS

Celtic knotwork patterns were developed as a form of artwork more than 1300 years ago and have elaborated upon the labyrinthine designs of old. The interlocking weaves form a fluid, continuous path that has no beginning and no end, representing the ongoing cycle of life.

Celtic knotwork originated in the middle of the 7th century when Irish monks returned from the Crusades bearing manuscripts from the Holy Land. Many similarities can be found between the precise geometric and interlocking motifs of the Middle East and the deftly woven knotwork that has become the defining characteristic of Irish arts and crafts. Illuminated manuscripts such as the *Book of Kells* and the *Lindisfarne Gospels* offer some of the most intricate examples of Celtic knotwork in the world.

A page from the illuminated manuscript, the Lindisfarne Gospels

Further developments in the artistic use of knot patterns are found in Byzantine architecture and book illumination, Islamic art, and medieval Russian illumination.

In symbolic terms, the unending path represents the continuous cycle of life, or love everlasting. Celtic knotwork incorporates icons such as horses, birds, dragons and people into artistically interwoven patterns.

In regions of Ireland and England, numerous stone crosses stand as artistic testaments to ancient Celtic culture. This elaborately detailed cross design, which predates Christianity, is called a Sun Cross, because the outer circle is believed to depict the Sun's radiance and life-giving properties. Some of the earliest Celtic crosses are adorned with inscriptions in runes.

Similarities between Celtic knotwork and Arabian tile patterns.

C. FILIPAK

The Realm of Faerie

Belief in faeries has existed from earliest times, and tales of faeries and their relations with humans have thrived in the literature and folklore of many cultures all over the world. It is believed by some that faeries are the ancestors of ancient pagan gods or nature deities. Other cultures identify faeries with the souls of the dead. Although they are commonly thought of as being magical creatures that bring good luck or simply revel in creating mischief, darker legends exist as well.

The ORIGIN OF FAERIES is historically accorded to the Old World Celtic beliefs of nations such as Ireland, Scotland, Wales and Brittany, with similar traditions held by the Teutonic peoples of Germany, as well as in Scandinavian countries. In Celtic lore faeries are generally believed to consist of two main social and political bodies: the Seelie and the Unseelie courts.

The SEELIE COURT is comprised of the most beautiful and heroic of the fae, also called the "Blessed Ones." These beings are kind, loving and helpful to mortals in many ways. They have also been known to be mischievous and capricious at times, but they do not intentionally cause harm to others as do those of the Unseelie Court. However, in the cases where faeries enter into love affairs with mortals, such liaisons frequently entail trickery or seduction and often end badly for those involved.

The UNSEELIE COURT is considered to be the wicked counterpart to the Seelie Court and includes mean-spirited and often fatal pranksters as well as harmful and dangerous creatures. These dark fae range in size and appearance, but their natures are similarly malevolent. Members of this court are believed by some to be former subjects of the Seelie Court who have fallen from grace. It is said that the Unseelie cannot reproduce, so they take human captives to make more of their kind.

The LOCATION OF THE REALM OF FAERIE varies depending on legend, but in any case, it has rarely, if ever, been visited by humans. Faeries are said to reside in an enchanted kingdom of their own, hidden by magic from the notice of mortals. They may dwell deep underground, beneath the sea, or in the darkest shadows of the forest.

Ancient Celtic peoples believed that faeries resided in *Annwn* or *Annwyn* (pronounced "anoon"), which is an equivalent of the Netherworld. It refers not to Heaven or Hell but to an underground realm inhabited by immortals, fair folk, demons or deities.

A derivative of Annwyn is the enchanted Isle of Avalon, of which much has been related since its literary introduction in 12th century Arthurian legends. Referred to as "The Fortunate Isle" and "The Isle of Apples," it is said to be a kind of paradise that produces all that one needs to flourish. Classical mythology says that the isle is presided over by Morgan le Fay, a kind sorceress and healer who leads a sisterhood of nine. Through the ages, Avalon became immortalized as the legendary site of King Arthur's stronghold, where he was taken for healing after battle and where the famous sword Excalibur was forged. Though it cannot be found on any map, some say that the true location of

Avalon is the Glastonbury Tor.

Tor literally means "rocky hill" or "peak" and it is a prominent site in Glastonbury, England, as well as the subject of many other curious legends. Celtic lore says that the Tor is hollow and that beneath it lies the entrance to the Underworld, the spirit world of Annwyn, and the Realm of Faerie. Thousands of years ago the Tor was surrounded by water, and for this reason it is believed to be the long lost Isle of Avalon. Other legends that surround the Tor have to do with the travels of Joseph of Arimathea and Jesus Christ, and it is even rumored to be the burial site of the Holy Grail.

Faeries can be either beautiful or ugly, good or evil, and they appear in many guises. Following is a list of the various kinds of faerie folk, their associations and descriptions.

Alven—Faeries of the Netherlands whose bodies are so light they are almost invisible. They travel through the air encased in a water bubble.

Banshee—A spirit faerie whose keening wail is an omen of death for a member of the family. The Irish *bean sidhe* (woman of the hills) is described as an old woman with eyes that are blood-red from constant weeping. She also appears as a beautiful young woman with a mournful visage and wildly flowing hair. She wears long gray robes and wanders about the grounds of the family homestead, her posture conveying great sadness and despair.

The Scottish version of this harbinger is the *caoineag* (wailing woman), or the *bean nighe* (washer at the ford), a woman who haunts nearby lakes and streams, washing phantom bloodstains from the grave clothes of those who are about to die. The *bean nighe* are believed to be the spirits of women who died giving birth and are doomed to do this work until the day their lives would have normally ended. They are said to have one nostril, one large protruding tooth, webbed feet and long hanging breasts. A mortal who is bold enough to sneak up to her while she is washing and suckle at her breast can claim to be her child. The mortal can then gain from her a wish.

Bean Tighe—Pronounced "ban-teeg," this Irish faerie is usually described as a small elderly woman, with a smiling and friendly demeanor. She is a kindhearted housekeeper and is especially helpful to tired and overworked mothers. This faerie loves children and will make sure they are taken care of, adjusting blankets, singing lullabies and closing drafty windows.

Boggart—A malicious and ill-tempered faerie whose bag of tricks includes making a mess of things, dumping over full drinking cups, slamming doors, blowing out candles, and tormenting household pets. They especially revel in the discomfort of sleeping babies, pinching them, pulling their hair or poking them until they wake screaming.

BOGIE—This mischievous but harmless spirit, also called a bugbear or bugaboo, dwells in dark places such as cellars, barns, attics, cupboards, hollow trees and caves. They create a vague sense of unease and enjoy spying on people and eavesdropping on their conversations.

BROWNIE—A good-natured, invisible faerie of Scottish lore that frequents farmsteads and will usually stay on with a family for as long as they are welcome. If well treated, they will help with minor chores while the family sleeps. However, if criticized, they will make much mischief. Servants would often leave bowls of milk as thanks to the brownies, but payment of anything other than food is considered a grave insult.

CHANGELING—An ill or deformed faerie child abandoned by the faeries in place of a healthy human child. Changelings can also be elderly faeries who are disguised as children, or inanimate objects, such as pieces of wood which take on the appearance of a child through faerie magic. Changelings are known for their wizened appearance, parchment-like skin, and dark eyes, which betray a wisdom far older than their apparent years. They are ill-tempered in nature, howling and screeching beyond the bounds of mortal endurance. Changelings may exhibit a full set of teeth and are said to have a ferocious appetite, though they are never satisfied and always appear scrawny, with legs as thin as chicken bones and clawed hands which are deformed and crooked as birds' talons.

CWN ANNWN—Pronounced "koon-anoon," means the "Hounds of Annwn," also called the "Hounds of Hell" by some. The Welsh tell of ghost dogs with snow-white fur and eyes like silver mirrors. The English call it the "Wild Hunt" and describe a pack of large black hounds with red eyes. These beasts snort fire and hunt humans. Running among them is the Huntmaster, a shadowy figure of a man with antlers upon his head.

DRYAD—Also called *hamadryads* or *sidhe draoi*, these are tree dwelling spirits from whom the female Druids took their name. Ancient Greek mythology tells of beautiful wood nymphs presiding over the forest as guardians and protectors of the woodlands.

DUENDE—The Spanish *duende* are faeries who appear as middle-aged women dressed in green robes and have long icicle-like fingers. They are extremely jealous of humans and are known to wreak havoc in the home, throwing things and moving furniture about. The *dwende* of Philippine folklore are usually helpful and friendly, but when offended they can cause sickness and even death.

Dullahan—Also referred to as the *Far Dorocha* or *Crom Dubh*. This is a headless rider mounted on a black steed, or sometimes driving a coach led by six headless horses. He carries his severed head aloft and uses a human spine as a whip. The horse sends out sparks and flames as it thunders through the night. Those who catch sight of him as he passes have a pail of blood thrown in their faces and are sometimes struck blind. Wherever this evil being stops, a mortal dies.

Dwarf—Also called *dwerger, dwergugh* or *duergarr*, these creatures are human-like in appearance, about half the size of a man, inhabiting caves or hollow trees. They can be hostile towards mankind, but can also perform small labors for them. Dwarves are exceptionally skilled at making beautiful, magical objects.

Elf—Also known as *elb, erl* or *mannikin*. In Norse legend, the elf is believed to be the spirit of the dead. Elves inhabit forests and mountains. They can be the fairest of all the fae, yet they can also be very ugly. Danish folklore describes them as beautiful creatures, but with hollow backs. Most are described as being of human size, though the Dutch mannikin is small and perfectly proportioned. Although they can be friendly to mankind, they are quite frequently vengeful and mischievous.

Erlking—Also called the *Erlkönig*, this malevolent elf king from Germanic legend haunts forests and lures people, especially children, to his death-realm. He is also said to lead the Wild Hunt.

Faun—The faeries of fertility, agriculture and wine. Like the *satyr* or Pan, the faun is part animal, with short horns and goat-like ears and the lower body of a deer. Unlike the satyr who is rather ugly and aggressive, the faun is very handsome and gentle. He plays a flute which attracts nymphs, but will run away when the satyr comes about, leaving the poor nymphs alone with the lascivious beast. A winegrower or farmer is lucky to have a faun on his property. His presence will ensure a good harvest and sweet grapes.

FyLgiaR—An Icelandic faerie which attaches itself to a human in life, yet is invisible until just before the person's death. Its appearance foretells the manner of death, whether it be painful or peaceful.

Gnome—A tiny dwarf-like creature that inhabits mines and quarries and is said to guard hidden treasures. Usually represented as misshapen or hunchbacked. Gnomes cannot bear the light of the sun, which would turn them to stone.

Goblin—Also known as a *hobgoblin* or *kobold* of Germanic folklore, this creature is a more grotesque variety of gnome. They are known to be playful, but their tricks are rarely harmful to people. A goblin's smile is said to curdle milk and cause fruit to fall from the trees. Their lesser pranks include hiding small objects, tipping over pails of milk and altering signposts.

Green Knight—A magical knight from the legendary tales of King Arthur and the Knights of the Round Table. He is so named because his skin, clothes, armor and weapons are all green. According to legend, he could replace his head if it was severed. The Green Knight challenges mortals to cut off his head. Those who accept his challenge find that after he has been beheaded the Green Knight does not die, instead he demands their head in return.

Green Ladies—These tree faeries are usually found in elm, oak, willow, and yew trees, and are easily offended if their trees are not treated with proper respect. Woodsmen may be wise to ask permission from them before cutting off a branch from one of their trees. In some parts of England, farmers still plant primroses at the feet of such trees in order to be rewarded with wealth and longevity. In Scotland, it is said that these ladies take the shape of trailing ivy and haunt a family just before someone's death.

Green Man—A legendary pagan deity who roams the woodlands and meadows of the British Isles. Also called Green Jack or Jack-in-the-Green, he is depicted as a horned man peering out of a mask of foliage, usually the sacred oak. The Green Man shares an affinity with the forest-dwelling faeries and is believed to possess the power to make rain.

Grim—A faerie whose wails foretell the death of the sick. At night, it would assume the form of a large black dog or owl and would set to howling below the window of the dying person.

Hag—A faerie from the British Isles, said to be the traces of the most ancient goddesses. The hag is regarded as the personification of winter. In the winter months she is usually old and very ugly looking. As the season changes though she becomes younger and more beautiful.

Kelpie—A treacherous and devilish faerie who lurks in the lakes and rivers of Scotland. It usually assumes the shape of a seahorse to befriend a human, then shifts into a bulbous-shaped creature with huge teeth and pointed ears, whereupon it drowns and eats the person.

Keshalyi—These are benevolent faeries of the Romany Gypsies of Transylvania. They live in the remote forests and mountains and resemble beautiful, small, fragile humans.

Lady of the Lake—The mysterious faerie queen who is said to inhabit the lake around the Isle of Avalon in the tales of King Arthur. This misty, supernatural figure, endowed with magic powers, bestowed the sword Excalibur unto King Arthur. According to legend she fostered the infant Lancelot in her underwater castle where he lived until manhood. She is also one of the faerie queens to take Arthur to Avalon after his death.

Lamiña—Evil faeries that live in the woods and on the shores of streams and rivers, usually appearing as part woman, part fish or bird.

Leanan Sidhe—The Irish *leanan sidhe* is known as the inspiration of poets and minstrels. She would roam the night, searching for romantic men to inspire, however, while in her embrace, their life force would be extinguished. On the Isle of Man, the *lliannan shee* is a vampiric spirit who attaches herself to a man, to whom she appears irresistibly beautiful yet invisible to all others. If he yields to her, the man is cursed body and soul.

Leprechaun—An Irish faerie, usually represented as a tiny old man in extravagant costume. They are said to possess buried pots of gold, the location of which may only be revealed upon their capture. However, they are crafty and elusive creatures, and have many ways to avoid giving up their gold. Leprechauns are known to carry two leather pouches; in one a silver shilling, a magical coin that returns to the purse each time it is paid out; in the other a gold coin which he uses to bribe his way out of difficult situations, but this coin usually turns to leaves or ashes once he has parted with it. Another trick involves granting three wishes, with a fourth wish used as a means to break the pact. Leprechauns are also called "fairy cobblers," for they make shoes for elves. The *cluricaun* is a more mischievous type, known to rob wine cellars and spend the entire night harassing and riding sheep and shepherds' dogs, leaving them panting and mud-drenched in the morning.

Lorelei—According to German legend, there was once a beautiful young maiden, named Lorelei, who threw herself headlong into the Rhine River in despair over a faithless lover. Upon her death she was transformed into a *siren*, similar to the beings of Greek mythology. She can be heard singing from the cliffs above the Rhine, where her hypnotic voice lures sailors to their death upon the rocks below.

Ly Erg—This dark faerie is a portent of death, however, one with whom there is yet a chance at life. It is said that he assumes the appearance of a warrior knight lying in wait for his mark on a lonely road. He hails the oncoming traveler by raising his crimson-red hand with a challenge to duel. If his challenge is met, the result is death for the human. His red hand is said to be the result of many years of bloodstains from those he has killed in combat.

Mab—Mistakenly referred to as a queen, she is more appropriately referred to as the "Midwife of Dreams" (Titania is actually wife of Oberon, King of the Faeries). Mab serves to deliver the dreams of men. It is said that she is so tiny that she travels in a coach led by insects. She is rumored to be a trickster who steals babies from their cribs and robs the secret dairies of young maidens. Mab is most likely derived from the Celtic goddess Maeve, who, according to 8th century Irish monks, was a fierce warrior and an avid lover of numerous kings.

THE CHINESE ZODIAC

The Chinese Zodiac consists of a twelve-year cycle, each year of which is named after a different animal that imparts distinct characteristics to those born during its year.

Many believe that the year of a person's birth is a primary factor in determining personality traits, physical and mental attributes, and degree of success and happiness throughout that person's lifetime.

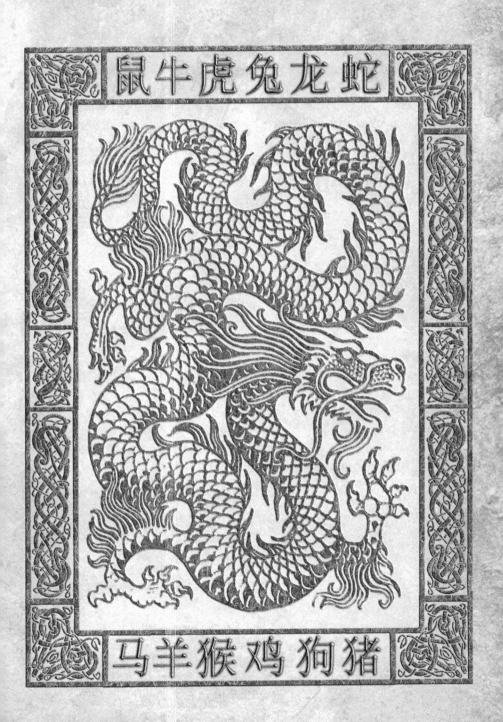

THE CHINESE LUNAR NEW YEAR

is the longest chronological record in history, dating from 2600 BC, when the Emperor Huang Ti introduced the first cycle of the Zodiac. Like the Western calendar, the Chinese calendar is a yearly one, however, it is based on the orbit of the moon rather than the Earth's orbit around the sun. Therefore, because the cycles of the moon are not perfectly synchronized with the solar year, the beginning of the lunar year can fall anywhere between late January and the middle of February.

THE CHINESE LUNAR CALENDAR

is made up of a cycle of sixty years, consisting of five cycles of twelve years. Each of the twelve years is named after an animal. Legend has it that an ancient Chinese emperor summoned all the creatures of the forest to a magnificent banquet to celebrate the New Year. Only twelve animals attended. The rat arrived first, followed by the ox, then the other animals, until finally the boar was the last to arrive. To honor the animals, the emperor named a year after each one in the order they arrived. It is believed that the sign ruling the year in which you are born designates the animal that hides in your heart, and has a profound influence on your personality.

RAT
1948, 1960, 1972, 1984, 1996, 2008, 2020

People born in the year of the Rat are noted for their charm and attraction. Their ambitions are great and they work hard to achieve their goals. They are often perfectionists. They are generous and good with money. They possess short tempers and are sometimes overly critical. They are most compatible with people born in the years of the Dragon and Monkey, and are least compatible with the sign of the Horse.

OX
1949, 1961, 1973, 1985, 1997, 2009, 2021

People born in the year of the Ox are patient and inspire confidence in others. They tend to be conservative and methodical, however, they are often demanding. They are natural leaders and also make skilled craftsmen. They are generally bright and alert. Although they are basically easy-going, they can be remarkably stubborn. They are most compatible with people born under the sign of the Snake and Rooster, and are least compatible with the sign of the Goat.

TIGER

1950, 1962, 1974, 1986, 1998, 2010, 2022

People born in the year of the Tiger are sensitive and intellectual. Although they are courageous, aggressive and direct, they can also be extremely short-tempered and stubborn. Because they are ruled by emotion, they have a tendency to be indecisive or make the wrong choices. Tigers are most compatible with Horses and Dogs, however, they have a tendency to clash with Monkeys.

RABBIT

1951, 1963, 1975, 1987, 1999, 2011, 2023

People born in the year of the Rabbit are extremely lucky. They are conservative and shy yet generous with their affections. They are considerate of others and make pleasant company. They are admired and trusted and very loyal to those closest to them. They are patient and well-spoken. They are most compatible with those born in the years of the Goat and Boar, and are least compatible with the sign of the Rooster.

DRAGON

1952, 1964, 1976, 1988, 2000, 2012, 2024

People born in the year of the Dragon have a passionate nature and are full of vitality and enthusiasm. They are gregarious and honest, making them quite popular. Dragons are brave to the extent of being foolhardy and have a fierce temper. They can be eccentric and quite demanding, and tend to be perfectionists. Those born under the sign of the Dragon are most compatible with Rats and Monkeys, but tend to clash with Dogs.

SNAKE

1953, 1965, 1977, 1989, 2001, 2013, 2025

People born in the year of the Snake are intuitive, intense, passionate and charming. They generally have a positive outlook and possess a healthy sense of humor. They tend to be a bit stingy, yet they have great sympathy for others and try to help those less fortunate. They are sometimes vain, fickle and obsessed with looks. They are most compatible with the Ox and Rooster and are least compatible with the Boar.

HORSE

1954, 1966, 1978, 1990, 2002, 2014, 2026

People born in the year of the Horse are cheerful, popular, perceptive and wise. They are very independent and rarely listen to advice. They have a strong sexual appeal and  are extremely passionate, but tend to be impatient, selfish and egotistical at times. They are hard working and good with money. Those born under the sign of the Horse are most compatible with Tigers and Dogs, and are least compatible with Rats.

GOAT

1955, 1967, 1979, 1991, 2003, 2015, 2027

Also known as the Ram or Sheep, those born under this sign are elegant and artistically creative. They are often timid,  but make charming company and loyal friends. They are wise, gentle and compassionate, however, they tend to be pessimistic and materialistic. Those born in the year of the Goat are compatible with Rabbits and Boars, and are least compatible with those born under the sign of the Ox.

MONKEY

1956, 1968, 1980, 1992, 2004, 2016, 2028

People born in the year of the Monkey are very intelligent, enthusiastic, and possess a clever wit. They are highly regarded and  influential. Although they can achieve great things, they are easily discouraged. They are strong willed, but tend to be skeptical and even suspicious of others. Those born under the sign of the Monkey are most compatible with the Dragon and Rat, and are least compatible with the Tiger.

ROOSTER

1957, 1969, 1981, 1993, 2005, 2017, 2029

People born in the year of the Rooster are extremely hard workers and shrewd in business. Though they quest for knowledge, they also tend to be dreamers. They fully devote themselves to their causes and are opinionated and often outspoken. They can be selfish and exhibit extravagant tastes. Those born under the sign of the Rooster are most compatible with Ox and Snake, and are least compatible with the Rabbit.

DOG

1958, 1970, 1982, 1994, 2006, 2018, 2030

People born in the year of the Dog are honest, dependable and possess a deep sense of loyalty. Though they are typically generous, they may also be selfish, stubborn and slightly eccentric at times. They are extremely critical and are noted for their sharp tongues. Those born under the sign of the Dog are compatible with the Horse and Tiger, and are least compatible with those born in the year of the Dragon.

BOAR

1959, 1971, 1983, 1995, 2007, 2019, 2031

Also known as the Pig, those born under this sign are noble and sincere. They exhibit tremendous fortitude and great honesty and make lifelong friends. They tend to set lofty goals for themselves and others, and are sometimes naive. They are soft spoken yet quick tempered. Those born under the sign of the Boar are most compatible with Rabbits and Goats, and are least compatible with the sign of the Snake.

The Science of
Phrenology

The science of Phrenology was
developed in the late 1700s
by physician Franz Joseph
Gall (1758-1828), who,
after years of dissecting and
studying the human brain,
concluded that it was the
"organ of the mind." Gall
theorized that there was a
direct correlation between the
shape of the brain and skull
and a person's abilities and
propensities. Phrenology
designates 39 separate
"organs" within the brain itself
that represent various human
traits, sentiments and
perceptions, and may be
interpreted by studying
particular regions of the skull.
Today, over two hundred years
later, the study of Phrenology
is still practiced.

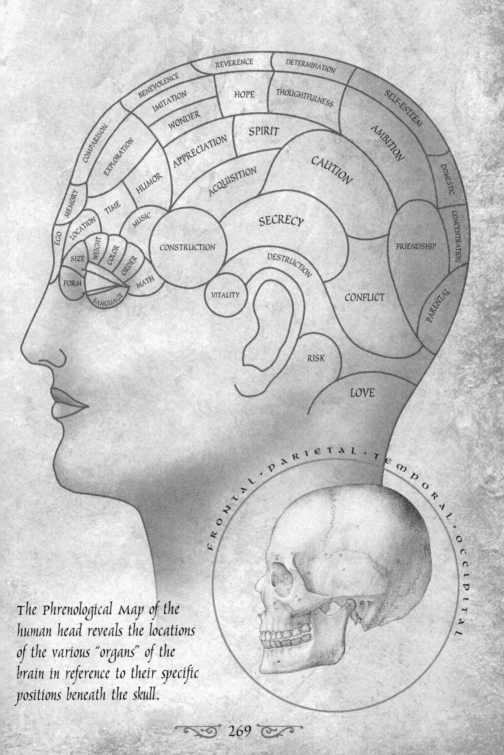

The Phrenological Map of the human head reveals the locations of the various "organs" of the brain in reference to their specific positions beneath the skull.

FRONTAL · PARIETAL · TEMPORAL · OCCIPITAL

Studying the Organs of the Mind

By studying the shape and development of the human skull, a skilled Phrenologist may be able to determine a person's propensities toward specific character traits. For an exact reading, calipers are used to measure the subject's skull, although it is also common for the Phrenologist to use their bare fingertips to locate bumps and indentations to determine the state of development of a particular area or "organ."

Extremely rounded areas or bumps indicate that a region is over developed, while flat areas and indentations are considered to be under developed. Following is a list of traits and abilities assigned to the various "organs."

Acquisition — the desire to possess, a tendency to collect things. *Over Developed:* selfish, miserly, hoarding, theft. *Under Developed:* foolish spending, or having little concept of value.

Ambition — the desire to excel in one's occupation or hobbies, and to achieve self-imposed goals. *Over Developed:* vanity, a constant thirst for praise from others, a disregard for others in one's quest for glory. *Under Developed:* laziness, low standards.

Appreciation — respect for that which is beautiful, poetic and artistic, a desire for the finer pleasures of intellect. *Over Developed:* a fussy, fastidious nature, extreme extravagance. *Under Developed:* a coarse nature with little taste for the arts.

Benevolence — the desire for the happiness and well-being of others, a charitable and sympathetic nature. *Over Developed:* an overindulgence of the appetites and fancies of others. *Under Developed:* extreme selfishness, a disinterest in other people, a lack of compassion.

Caution — discretion, prudence, the ability to consider surrounding circumstances before taking decisive action. *Over Developed:* a false sense of security, a tendency to act recklessly or to put oneself in harm's way. *Under Developed:* an excessively timid nature, unfounded fears.

Color — the ability to perceive colors, values and hues in relation to one another.

Comparison — the ability to draw conclusions based on the analysis of similarities and differences.

CONCENTRATION — the ability to focus clearly on a train of thought. *Over Developed:* a tendency to over think or dwell on emotions and ideas and neglect outside concerns. *Under Developed:* a tendency to daydream.

CONFLICT — the combative nature of the human spirit. *Over Developed:* a quarrelsome disposition regarding all matters, a tendency to provoke fights. *Under Developed:* gives in easily to the wills of others.

CONSTRUCTION — a proficiency in manual pursuits, art and science. *Over Developed:* a diligent worker, but one who aspires to achieve impossible goals. *Under Developed:* spineless, lazy, non-productive.

DESTRUCTION — the desire to destroy animate and inanimate objects. *Over Developed:* cruelty, murder, a desire to torment, a tendency to rage, harshness and severity in speech and writing. *Under Developed:* a nature given to procrastination, a tendency to cling to useless things.

DETERMINATION — perseverance, a firm and persistent nature. *Over Developed:* a tenacious, obstinate and unreasonable nature, prone to stubbornness. *Under Developed:* hesitant, indecisive, prone to infatuation with those of a stronger will.

DOMESTIC — a love of spouse, family and all the comforts of home. *Over Developed:* an aversion to change of residence or travel of any kind. *Under Developed:* the need to travel, escape and roam the world.

EGO — the sense of self, individuality. *Over Developed:* narcissism, vanity, a lack of sincere interest in others. *Under Developed:* a tendency to copy others, the inability to form one's own opinions.

EXPLORATION — the desire to make new discoveries and the ability to understand relationships between cause and effect.

FORM — the ability to perceive and memorize shapes and forms.

FRIENDSHIP — loyalty toward those closest to you. *Over Developed:* naive to the faults of others, overly trusting, an attachment to individuals who may pose a bad influence. *Under Developed:* self-serving and overly ambitious at the expense of others.

Hope — an expectant, cheerful and optimistic outlook on life. *Over Developed:* faulty speculation, a tendency to put too much reliance on others, extreme optimism. *Under Developed:* incredulous, entrusting and pessimistic.

Humor — a witty nature disposed to mirth with the ability to enjoy the funny side of life. *Over Developed:* indicative of a caustic and ill-timed wit, sometimes combined with malicious sarcasm. *Under Developed:* taking oneself and others too seriously, a brooding nature.

Imitation — the ability to mimic the manners, gestures, and actions of others, thereby the ability to learn through example. *Over Developed:* a subservient nature, lacking in assertiveness. *Under Developed:* a slow learner, the tendency to make the same mistakes more than once.

Language — the ability for coherent verbal expression.

Location — the ability to perceive and memorize relative position.

Love — sexual attraction or physical love. *Over Developed:* denotes a lack of physical and mental harmony and problems dealing in matters of love. *Under Developed:* denotes a preoccupation with affairs of the heart.

Math — the ability to count and utilize numbers in calculations.

Memory — the ability to recall past observations.

Music — the ability to appreciate melody, harmony and rhythm.

Order — the ability to recognize a logical, physical arrangement; a methodical, tidy nature.

Parental — the instinct for parenting and the love of children, also the caring and tenderness for animals. *Under Developed:* apathy or neglect for a child. *Over Developed:* pampering and spoiling children.

Reverence — the proper respect for those worthy of it and holding spiritual matters in high esteem. *Over Developed:* a senseless respect for unworthy objects, subservience, superstitious awe, religious mania. *Under Developed:* a lack of respect for anything or anyone.

Risk — the capacity for self-preservation and the natural desire to live. *Over Developed:* this may indicate hesitancy or cowardly behavior. *Under Developed:* a reckless disregard for personal safety; an extreme deficiency may indicate a propensity toward self-destruction.

Secrecy — tact, prudence, and the capacity to keep things to oneself. *Over Developed:* cunning, evasive, deceitful, or sneaky in nature. *Under Developed:* blunt and outspoken to the point of being abrasive, highly opinionated.

Self-Esteem — self-respect, dignity and independence; an appreciation for one's own talents and a realistic view of imperfections. *Over Developed:* a haughty, egotistical nature, feelings of superiority. *Under Developed:* feelings of inferiority and worthlessness.

Size — the ability to discern the measure of space and gauge dimension and distance.

Spirit — that which motivates and inspires one to reach difficult goals in the face of adversity.

Thoughtfulness — a conscientious nature, a respect for rights, the desire for honesty, justice and truth. *Over Developed:* strict censorship, remorse or self-condemnation, an adherence to ignorantly embraced principles. *Under Developed:* little or no sense of duty and obligation, an uncaring nature.

Time — the ability to perceive chronology and duration.

Vitality — physical well-being, health, nutrition, energy, lively appetite. *Under Developed:* an unhealthy appetite, a propensity to deprive one's body of proper nourishment. *Over Developed:* gluttony and drunkenness or an addiction to sensual pleasures.

Weight — the ability to perceive gravity, momentum, and resistance.

Wonder — the admiration of the unexpected, the grand, the wonderful, and the extraordinary. *Over Developed:* an overly superstitious belief in miracles, prodigies, and other fantastical things. *Under Developed:* a skeptical and materialistic outlook.

FORTUNE TELLING WITH PLAYING CARDS

Hold a deck of playing cards in both hands and concentrate upon a question that concerns you deeply. Shuffle the deck three times, each time asking your question out loud. Lay the cards face down and cut the deck three times. Turn the top card face up to reveal your fortune. Consult the Oracle of the Cards on the following pages to interpret what your future holds.

SPADES

MYSTERY • DANGER

HEARTS

LOVE • HEALTH

DIAMONDS

WEALTH • PRESTIGE

CLUBS

LUCK • WISDOM

ORACLE OF THE CARDS

SPADES

A ♠ This card foretells of danger.

2 ♠ This card foretells of a reunion.

3 ♠ This card advises to trust in fate.

4 ♠ This card warns to beware unsuspected enemies.

5 ♠ This card foretells of illness or loss.

6 ♠ This card foretells of an important discovery.

7 ♠ This card predicts you will prevail over a foe.

8 ♠ This card warns of dark forces at work.

9 ♠ This card predicts success in a current endeavor.

10♠ This card signifies turmoil.

J ♠ This card advises to expect the unexpected.

Q ♠ This card denotes someone desires you from afar.

K ♠ This card foretells triumph over adversity.

DIAMONDS

A ♦ This card designates respect.

2 ♦ This card foretells of a successful venture.

3 ♦ This card advises caution. Take no risks.

4 ♦ This card foretells of financial gain.

5 ♦ This card foretells of a journey or change of residence.

6 ♦ This card foretells you will face adversity.

7 ♦ This card designates good fortune.

8 ♦ This card denotes loyalty and trust.

9 ♦ This card is a very positive omen.

10♦ This card foretells of bright new prospects.

J ♦ This card signifies an inheritance.

Q ♦ This card predicts long-term success.

K ♦ This card designates prosperity and acclaim.

HEARTS

A ♥ This card foretells you will be lucky in love.

2 ♥ This card foretells of a harmonious union.

3 ♥ This card signifies betrayal.

4 ♥ This card foretells of new love on the horizon.

5 ♥ This card designates romantic turmoil.

6 ♥ This card foretells of a separation.

7 ♥ This card denotes beauty and good health.

8 ♥ This card foretells of a rival for your affections.

9 ♥ This card advises a change in your appearance or habits.

10♥ This card foretells that you will attain your heart's desire.

J ♥ This card denotes secret passions.

Q ♥ This card signifies true love.

K ♥ This card designates self-confidence.

CLUBS

A ♣ This card advises to follow your intuition.

2 ♣ This card is an omen of bad luck.

3 ♣ This card denotes accomplishment and fulfillment.

4 ♣ This card signifies that you possess the keys to success.

5 ♣ This card foretells of a journey.

6 ♣ This card predicts you will prosper from an act of kindness.

7 ♣ This card is an omen of good luck.

8 ♣ This card signifies calamity.

9 ♣ This card advises take nothing for granted.

10♣ This card advises a change of strategy.

J ♣ This card foretells of a reward for your efforts.

Q ♣ This card signifies revelry and celebration.

K ♣ This card designates great strength and wisdom.

FINDING YOUR SOULMATE

The belief that we all have one person who is our perfect romantic match is an age-old concept that is held to be true by countless people. The ancient Egyptians developed ways to recognize Soulmates who had been separated by death and reincarnated to live again.

AURA OF INFLUENCE

SPIRITUAL BELIEFS

EMOTIONAL STABILITY

PHYSICAL APPEARANCE

TRAVEL

ROMANCE

INTELLECT

RECREATION

CAREER GOALS

FAMILY AND HOME

FINANCIAL GAINS

EARTH   AIR   WATER   FIRE

SPHERES OF INFLUENCE

Rank the Spheres of Influence in the order of their importance to you and number then from 1 to 10, with 1 being the most important, and 10 being the least important. Compare your list with your partner's choices. If your first and last choices are the same or close, then you will have much in common and therefore be compatible. If, however, your lists produce opposite results, you may find disappointment later in the relationship.

SHARED MINDSETS

The object of this exercise is to determine how well you and your partner know one another's likes and dislikes. It may also indicate if you are able to pick up on each other's thoughts and moods. Both you and your partner should begin by secretly selecting three random hieroglyphs that appeal to you from the choices above. Then choose three that you don't particularly like. Write them on a sheet of paper, keeping them from each other's view. Then try to pick the glyphs that your partner chose as their three likes and three dislikes. While one of you is guessing, the other should try to send a mental image of each glyph in turns.

A perfect score is 6 out of 6 correct, and indicates you know your partner well. A score of 3 out of 3 for the likes, but 0 out of 3 correct on the dislikes is still very good, but may indicate that you need to pay closer attention to your partner's tastes, or it may also indicate that your partner needs to communicate more clearly about his or her preferences. When it comes to simple things, like music or art, it's easy for people to tell each other what they like, but when the issue is more personal, it's not always that comfortable explaining a dislike, so do this in a kind and friendly way.

COMPATIBILITY CHART

In the following chart, find the number assigned to each personal attribute. Tally the numbers that pertain to you from each of the 7 categories, then in a separate column, do the same for the person you are interested in. Add up each column separately to arrive at two final scores. Subtract the smaller number from the larger number, then refer to the following list to determine your level of compatibility. This will enable you to find out what your chances are of having a secure relationship, and if it is one of passion, close friendship, or contrasting personalities.

PRIMARY HAND	RIGHT 5	LEFT 1		
AGE	UNDER 18 8	18–30 5	OVER 30 2	
HEIGHT	SHORT 9	AVERAGE 5	TALL 1	
EYE COLOR	BROWN 5	BLUE 4	GREEN 3	
HAIR COLOR	BLONDE 3	BROWN 5	BLACK 7	RED 8
ELEMENT	EARTH 2	AIR 7	WATER 6	FIRE 3
MAIN INTEREST	PHYSICAL 3	SPIRITUAL 6	INTELLECTUAL 8	CREATIVE 7

FIND YOUR ELEMENT

The astrological signs of the Zodiac are divided into four groups to represent the elements of Earth, Air, Water and Fire. Find the number in the chart that corresponds to your element.

EARTH—Capricorn, Taurus, Virgo
AIR—Aquarius, Gemini, Libra
WATER—Cancer, Pisces, Scorpio
FIRE—Aries, Leo, Sagittarius

0–5   SOULMATES: A very rare perfect match signifying two people who are destined to be together forever. Arguments are rare. Close friendship, romantic bliss and extreme passion co-exist in this union.

6–10   LOVERS: A loving and passionate relationship with the potential for some minor disagreements, but overall a secure and caring union with binding mutual interests.

11–15   GOOD FRIENDS: Deep trust and security with secrets. Some romantic interest may blossom with time, but deep emotions are usually kept at bay.

16–20   FRIENDS: Similar interests, enjoying each other's company, but not at the exclusion of other possibilities.

21–25   LUST: A wild fling, pure physical attraction with no real basis for a long lasting relationship. Fun but short-lived.

26–30   OPPOSITES ATTRACT: Based more on intellectual attraction, a high degree of competition and verbal debate may draw people together more than any physical trait. Diversely opposed personalties create a curious attraction.

31–35   FIRE & ICE: Nothing in common, quarrels to be expected, boredom and irritation, and though matches are rare, it could lead to bitter feelings if the relationship doesn't last.

The Kabbalah

For thousands of years the mystical practice of Kabbalah has brought illumination, inner peace and prosperity to those who follow its path. The ancient rite teaches us to transcend the tribulations and limitations of the physical world to achieve spiritual enlightenment.

1
KETER
The Crown
2
CHOCHMAH
Wisdom
3
BINAH
Understanding
DAAT
Knowledge
(hidden)
4
CHESED
Kindness
5
GEVURAH
Strength
6
TIFERET
Beauty
7
NETZACH
Victory
8
HOD
Splendor
9
YESOD
Foundation
10
MALCHUT
Kingdom
Beth ב
Aleph א
Daleth ד
Cheth ח
Zain ז
Hé ה
Vau ו
Gimel ג
Teth ט
Lamed ל
Yod י
Mem מ
Kaph כ
Ayin ע
Samech ס
Nun נ
Pé פ
Resh ר
Tzaddi צ
Shin ש
Qoph ק
Tau ת
INTELLECT
EMOTION
ENERGY
THE PILLAR OF SEVERITY
THE PILLAR OF MERCY

THE HISTORY AND BASIS OF KABBALAH

Kabbalah (also Qabalah, favored by occultists, and Cabala, a Christian spelling) is a complex Hebrew spiritual philosophy, a form of mysticism that incorporates and elaborates upon religious beliefs and meditative practices. Kabbalah, meaning "to receive," implies that each of us is capable of receiving wisdom and knowledge from a divine source. Many modern practitioners of Kabbalah believe that separate minds can essentially come together as one, and in doing so transcend that which is material in order to focus on things that concern and affect the very nature of existence.

There are two main areas of Kabbalistic study—the theoretical and the practical. The theoretical Kabbalists strive to understand and describe the nature of God. They are apt to spend much of their time in prayer and meditation while searching for hidden meanings in the Torah. They do not necessarily strive to change the physical world, but seek to understand it, and in doing so, they become more in tune with the spiritual forces of the universe. Practical Kabbalists are more interested in producing tangible effects on the world around them. Their practices might involve elements of magic, the construction of amulets, and even the exorcising of demons, but with very strict guidelines that require the invocation of the divine and strict adherence to natural laws. The one firm rule that governs any practice of Kabbalah is reverence and respect for the divine.

The Torah, the Hebrew bible, is comprised of five books written by Moses: Genesis, Exodus, Leviticus, Numbers and Deuteronomy. Tradition holds that there are four levels of meaning within the Torah, ranging from the literal message to a secret or embedded message, which is where Kabbalah comes into play. Originally passed along through oral tradition, Kabbalistic theories were eventually set in writing with the Sefer Yetzirah ("Book of Formation"), an enigmatic text written sometime between the 2nd and 6th centuries that proposed to explain God's creation of the universe, and the Zohar ("Book of Splendor"), written in the 12th century, which attempted to answer profound religious questions involving the nature and will of God. These ancient books are considered by most to be essential in fully understanding and implementing the secrets of Kabbalah.

To understand Kabbalah, one must have at least a rudimentary knowledge of the Hebrew alphabet. In Jewish culture, words are believed to have power, and the Hebrew script itself is considered sacred. Traditionally, one or more of the names of God is invoked during ritual or inscribed on an amulet in order to give it power. This name might be any one of the Hebrew words used in prayer to address or distinguish the divine. One of the most revered names that appears in the Torah and which is used on many amulets is יהוה (YHVH in English). This configuration is referred to as a tetragrammaton, and is sometimes meditated upon as the Kabbalist rearranges the letters to form different permutations of the name. Practitioners of Kabbalah who memorize and cite these names are referred to as Ba'al Shem Tov, or "Master of Names."

THE HOLY 72-PART NAME

This sacred name is made out of 72 triads of letters, and is one of the most powerful names a Kabbalist might use. It is derived from the book of *Exodus*, each line of which has 72 letters. Legend holds that this name of God was revealed to Moses at the Burning Bush, and that it was invoked to part the Red Sea.

כהת	אכא	ללה	מהש	עלם	סיט	ילי	והו
הקם	הרי	מבה	יזל	ההע	לאו	אלד	הזי
וזהו	מלה	ייי	נלך	פהל	לוו	כלי	לאו
ושר	לכב	אום	ריי	שאה	ירת	האא	נתה
יין	רהע	וזעם	אני	מנד	כוק	להו	יוזו
מיה	עשל	ערי	סאל	ילה	וול	מיכ	ההה
פוי	מבה	נית	גנא	עמם	הוש	דני	והו
מוזי	ענו	יהה	ומב	מצר	הרח	ייל	נמם
מום	היי	יבם	ראה	וזבו	איע	מנק	דמב

THE TEN SEFIROT AND THE TREE OF LIFE

In their attempt to explain the nature of the divine, the creation of the universe, and mankind's place in it, the ancient mystics used various metaphors in order to better illustrate that which was otherwise indescribable and incomprehensible. They also devised a diagram to visually communicate their concept.

According to Kabbalah, divine essence cannot be described or even conceived of in human terms, nor can one interact directly with the divine, for it is immaterial and infinite. Kabbalah theory states that this essence, known as *ein sof*, meaning "without end," interacts with our material world through ten emanations, or lights, known as the *sefirot* (*sefirah* being the singular form of this word). The sefirot act as a conduit through which the divine interacts with our world. They are depicted as circles, interconnected by the various paths of the Tree of Life.

Divine will travels from the topmost sefirah called *Keter* and flows down until it comes to the material realm of *Malchut*, where it can be received by mankind in some recognizable way. The concept is like that of a prism as it refracts a beam of light into a spectrum of individual colors. Though separate, the beams all flow from one source of light, and may also be redirected back to that source.

The sefirot are shown on the Tree of Life, which is in some ways a map of Creation. Perhaps, it might be considered a list of the required intellectual, emotional and physical ingredients required for Creation. Each sefirah corresponds to a quality or trait that is associated with the divine. The uppermost sefirot are associated with intellect, the middle with emotion, the lower with energy and matter, and are divided into triads.

The First Triad — Intellect

The first sefirah, *Keter*, is called the Crown, and symbolizes a state of enlightenment and compassion that is above the comprehension of mere mortals. There also exists a "hidden light" called *Daat*, meaning knowledge. Daat is not considered one of the ten sefirot. Its hidden state implies hidden knowledge—attainable yet hidden from those who are not yet able to receive it. The second sefirah, *Chochmah*, is associated with male aspects, fatherhood, potential, intent, and conscious intellect. *Binah*, the third sefirah, is associated with feminine traits, motherhood, creativity and comprehension.

The Second Triad — Emotion

The fourth sefirah, *Chesed*, concerns love, kindness and mercy. Chesed helps to counterbalance the fifth sefirah, *Gevurah*, which symbolizes power, force and severity. It also represents judgment and the strength to fairly but firmly impose sanctions or exact punishment, if need be. The sixth sefirah is *Tiferet*, which symbolizes beauty, both physical and spiritual, and signifies inspiration.

The Third Triad — Energy

The seventh sefirah, *Netzach*, is associated with perpetual force and other dominant forms of energy. The eighth sefirah, *Hod*, is associated with glory, majesty and praise, or prayer. It represents submissive forms of energy. *Yesod*, the ninth sefirah, acts to stabilize, collect and distribute the flow of energy toward the physical realm and into the last of the Sefirot, *Malchut*, which alone represents all that is material and finite in our world, the earth, our kingdom.

SEFIROT	MEANING	DIVINE NAME	ARCHANGEL
Keter	The Crown	Ehieh	Metatron
Chochmah	Wisdom	Yah	Ratziel
Binah	Understanding	Yhvh Elohim	Tzaphkiel
Chesed	Kindness	El	Tzadkiel
Gevurah	Strength	Elohim Gibor	Khamael
Tiferet	Beauty	Yhvh Eloah ve-Daath	Michael
Netzach	Victory	Yhvh Tzabaoth	Uriel
Hod	Splendor	Elohim Tzaboath	Raphael
Yesod	Foundation	Shaddai El Chai	Gabriel
Malchut	Kingdom	Adonai ha-Aretz	Sandalphon

The 22 Paths

The ten Sefirot are connected by twenty-two paths, each being mapped to one of the 22 letters of the Hebrew alphabet.

א	Aleph	A		ט	Teth	T		פ	Pé	P, Ph, F
ב	Beth	B		י	Yod	Y, J		צ	Tzaddi	Tz, X
ג	Gimel	G		כ	Kaph	K		ק	Qoph	Q
ד	Daleth	D		ל	Lamed	L		ר	Resh	R
ה	Hé	H, E		מ	Mem	M		ש	Shin	Sh
ו	Vau	U, V		נ	Nun	N		ת	Tau	Th
ז	Zain	Z		ס	Samech	S				
ח	Cheth	Ch		ע	Ayin	I, O				

The Pillars

The Sefirot that run up and down the left side are referred to as the Pillar of Severity. Those on the right side make up the Pillar of Mercy. The concept is one of perpetual balance. This ideal is exemplified in the relationship between *Chesed* (kindness) and *Gevurah* (strength); without mercy to balance power, our world would be unjust and violent. Likewise, with no force to give one direction and purpose, our existence would be very boring and unproductive. The pillars symbolize what we now know of the right and left sectors of the human brain. Those who exhibit more creativity and emotion are said to use their right brain, while the more analytical personality types tend to use their left. In each case, a balance is ideal, and may validate the old cliché that "opposites attract." What is amazing is that this concept was born millennia ago, long before the brain was charted by scientists.

THE FOUR WORLDS

To make the Kabbalistic system even more complex, The Tree of Life is thought to exist in four realities, planes or worlds. The Four Worlds are: *Atziluth* (the archetypal world), *Briah* (the creative world), *Yetzirah* (the formative world), and *Assiah* (the material world). Each world determines how much and what type of influence is exerted upon each Sefirot.

In some Kabbalistic systems the Sefirot are also assigned an Archangel, an angelic host, a color, a chakra, and a ruling planet. Modern mystics have also drawn correlations between the Kabbalah and the Tarot—the twenty-two paths and the twenty-two cards of the Major Arcana, the ten Sefirot and the ten number cards of the Minor Arcana, the Four Worlds and four suits or court cards of the Tarot.

WORLD	ELEMENT	ATTRIBUTE	TAROT SUIT
Atziluth	Fire	Archetypal	Wands
Briah	Water	Creative	Cups
Yetzirah	Air	Formative	Swords
Assiah	Earth	Material	Pentacles

Angels & Demons

Kabbalists believe that some angels are created as "forms of thought" called *maggidim*. Such creation involves strict observance of holy rituals. These angels may reveal unto the individual future events and other universal mysteries. Some maggidim are truthful, such as those created from readings of the Torah or through holy observances performed perfectly and selflessly. Other maggidim may be misleading, mixing truth and falsehood. The reason for this is that some ulterior motive in an observance created an imperfect angel that speaks both good and evil.

Whenever possible, Kabbalistic procedures were thoroughly planned in advance, taking into consideration favorable Sabbath days or astrological occurrences, when it was believed that spirits of evil would be at their weakest. Sometimes preparations would last for days, typically involving fasting, ritual cleansing, abstinence from certain activities, meditation, and prayer. Incantations or written amulets had to invoke God. Angels might also be called upon. Biblical passages were quoted. Finally, the request would be made, concluding with the name of the affected, identifying them as the son or daughter of their mother (as opposed to identifying them with the father, which was used for legal matters). Oftentimes, the incantation was repeated three, seven, or nine times.

The *Ba'al Shem* might spit before or after the ritual, particularly after fasting, which was considered to be a potent weapon against evil spirits and demons. He

might also protect himself or the affected with one or more magical circles. Virgin elements were often required as well, such as soil that had never been plowed and fresh water from a natural spring or river.

The person's dwelling and belongings might be examined for signs of evil. Knots in fringe or cords might indicate the existence of a binding spell. Ritually unclean food or damaged holy items would create an unclean environment, providing an open invitation to demons.

Lilith—Queen of Demons

It is said that Lilith was the first woman, created along with Adam, just as all the animals, male and female, were made at one time. Lilith argued that she was Adam's equal in every respect, and as such she refused to obey him. Legend says that she grew wings and flew away from the Garden of Eden to hide in a cave by the sea, where she had relations with demons, and bore all manner of demonic offspring.

When Adam complained to God, He sent three angels, Sanvi, Sansanvi and Semangelaf, to bring Lilith back to Eden. The angels threatened that her children would be killed if she did not return to Adam. Lilith refused, and God punished her accordingly then gave Adam the docile Eve as his mate. Lilith in turn vowed to kill their children.

Lilith and her children, the *incubi* and *succubi*, seduced mortals in their dreams and produced other hybrid demons. To this day some believe that Lilith and her daughters, the *lilim* or *lilot*, remain jealous of the human children of Adam and Eve, and will attack mothers and their young, unless repelled by the holy names of the three angels. In medieval times women in labor would wear amulets to protect them from Lilith.

More recently, people have become sympathetic toward Lilith, viewing her as a victim. It has been suggested that Lilith represented early feminist views and was created by men to frighten women into assuming a submissive role in society. Later myths vilified Lilith as the Queen of Demons and mother to all creatures of darkness.

The Golem

The most revered implementation of practical Kabbalah is that which involves the creation of artificial life. A golem is a magical servant resembling a human that has been brought to life by means of an ancient ritual spell. The word golem implies something unfinished—a body without a soul. The ability to create this thing represented the culmination of spiritual wisdom, proving that if a man was pious and righteous enough, he could create life. According to popular Jewish lore, a golem served as a protector against injustice.

In creating a golem, a mixture of virgin soil and water was prepared and molded into the general shape of a man. The Kabbalist circled the body, reciting sacred names, and the body gradually took on more human qualities. When the golem was complete, it was awakened by means of placing a word or a name on its forehead, forearm, or in its mouth. Examples of such words used are: Adam, the name of the first man, who was also created from the earth, or the word *emet*, meaning "truth." When it came time to put down the golem, the first letter of these words was erased. Adam becomes *dam* (blood); *emet* becomes *met* (dead). If a name of God had been written on a parchment and placed in the mouth, it was simply removed.

DIVINATION WITH COINS AND DICE

Long before the discovery and development of the known sciences, our ancestors created numerous ways to attempt to divine the future. Interpreting signs and patterns by casting common objects such as coins and dice was believed to enable people to commune with the mysterious forces of the spirit realm in order to glimpse the unknown.

GYROMANCY

The traditional practice of this method of divination requires a person to walk on a
circle of letters until they become dizzy. It is said that the letters they stumble
upon will provide the answer to their question. A much more practical method that
was popularized in the Victorian Era uses a coin, spinning it upon a circle of
letters drawn on paper, similar in nature to the design of a Ouija board. A
question is asked and the coin is spun, then each time the coin falls upon a letter,
it is noted. Continue spinning the coin until the entire message becomes clear.

Cleromancy: Divination with dice. This practice, also known as *Astragalomancy*, is believed to have originated with the ancient Greeks who foretold future events by "casting lots" using carved knuckle-bones of animals, called *astragaloi*. Throughout the years the method was refined to utilize ivory dice thrown into a circle.

INSTRUCTIONS: Draw a 12" circle on the ground. Use two dice when asking a specific yes or no question, three dice for a more generalized reading. Shake the dice while silently concentrating on your question, then toss them into the circle. If after throwing the dice, one rolls outside the circle, it should be ignored and the fortune read for the remaining lot. If two roll out, the dice should be re-thrown. If all the dice roll out of the circle again, no fortune may be read this day; try again the following day. If using three dice, and one die lands atop another and stays there, it foretells of a gift or something of value.

Add the number of spots facing up on the dice and refer to the following list of answers. It is believed that whatever is predicted by the dice will begin to come true within nine days.

TWO DICE ANSWERS:
1. Yes (if one die falls outside the circle).
2. No.
3. Take great care in handling this situation.
4. Don't act rashly; think before proceeding further.
5. A promise of good fortune.
6. The outcome of your current situation looks very favorable.
7. It is advised to continue along your present path.
8. Be patient, a positive result is soon to come.
9. Your current venture will be successful.
10. Expect some disappointing news.
11. Your current direction indicates trouble ahead.
12. There is a slim chance for success.

THREE DICE ANSWERS:
1. Foretells of family strife.
2. Time to re-evaluate your position on the matter.
3. Expect a pleasant surprise.
4. Beware an unexpected bit of bad luck.
5. Your wish will soon come true.
6. Expect a loss of something of value.
7. Foretells stress in a relationship.
8. Indicates an unfair amount of disapproval.
9. Love and romance will be forthcoming.
10. Foretells of the birth of an idea or person.
11. Foretells of a separation.
12. Good news will soon be arriving.
13. Indicates a period of grief or stress.
14. You will meet a new friend that will offer help.
15. Avoid temptation, lest it be your downfall.
16. Indicates a journey with favorable results.
17. Business plans may change, but favorably so.
18. An extremely good omen.

Cycle of the Seasons

The Ancients recognized seasons and celestial events as important markers in their calendar. Druids, Celts, Romans, and many other past civilizations have celebrated such events with festivals in honor of various deities, with the hope of ensuring the benevolent favor of gods and goddesses.

WHEEL OF THE YEAR

The wheel symbolizes the processes of life—birth, growth, death and rebirth—as a neverending cycle. This form of illustrating the calendar was developed thousands of years ago. Nature itself is the primary focus. Each of the four seasons are represented as are four unique celestial events. These eight days have been celebrated by the Celts and other closely associated cultures for well over 2,000 years. Such festivals were the very early precursors to many of the world's currently observed religious holidays. Following is a description of each festival, their evolution and cultural associations.

ANCIENT DEITIES

To understand the relationship between the pagan festivals of old and the established modern holidays, it is necessary to understand the events that shaped the ancients' calendar and the beliefs that once flourished throughout Northern Europe. The personification of Nature was depicted in various forms depending on one's culture. For many Germanic and Scandinavian tribes (Celts, Druids, Vikings) and other North European clans, the events and seasons of the year were described almost like a recurring fairy tale. Aspects of seasonal changes were attributed to a God and Goddess, or King and Queen, in order to explain the mysterious processes of life—birth, growth, union, aging and death—with the added prospect of rebirth with the New Year.

Each of the deities were given multiple roles to play throughout the year. During the early part of the year, the Goddess or Queen represented the Maiden (a young virgin). As the seasons passed, she matured into Woman and Mother (lover and life-giver), and with the coming winter, she aged to become the Crone (old woman). The God or King transformed too, from his rebirth as the Divine Child to his maturity into Consort and King (lover and husband). His union with the Goddess sowed the seeds for the creation of the Divine Child, whose rebirth at Yule would start the cycle all over again. The Old King would die or be sacrificed to make way for the arrival of the Child (the God/King reborn). The Crone would transform again into the Maiden. And on, and on... This dramatic story illustrated how the cycle of life, death and rebirth continued each year.

THE PAGAN CALENDAR

The methods used in past times to determine days and months differ from what we know today. The Celtic calendar, for example was based on nights, not days. The Celts believed that day followed night, that the world was born in darkness, then came light. Therefore, it was determined that a "day" began at sunset the preceding evening and ended at sunset on the "day" in question, rather than counting the hours from midnight to midnight as we do today. For this reason, many of the festivals are celebrated throughout the preceding night into the following day.

Yule, Ostara, Litha and *Mabon* are celebrated during significant solar days: the two *solstices*, the longest day and the shortest day of the year, and the two *equinoxes*, when the hours of day and night are equal. These four days, also called "quarter days," separate the light and dark halves of the year, and indicate when the aspects of light and dark are perfectly balanced. Due to their relation with the sun, and hence a sun god, these days are considered to be of a more masculine nature.

Samhain, Imbolc, Beltane, and *Lughnasadh* celebrate the changing of the seasons and the cycle of harvest. These "cross-quarter days" occur midway between the solar days and are tracked by lunar events. Traditionally, these lunar festivals (also called "fire festivals") began on the eve of a full moon with the revelry continuing unabated throughout the night, and all day long until sunset of the following day. Because they are related to the moon, and hence the Goddess, these days are considered to be feminine in nature.

Because pagan festivals coincide with celestial events such as solar and lunar positions in the sky, the dates are apt to shift slightly from year to year. After the Julian calendar was established around 45 B.C. (reformed as the Gregorian calendar in 1582, which we still adhere to today), some of the festivals were assigned specific dates based on the recorded celestial event at that time. One prime example is the close proximity of Yule (December 21) and Christmas (December 25). Yule was always celebrated on the eve of the winter solstice. According to the Julian calendar the solstice occurred on December 25th, which is December 21 on the Gregorian calendar. Unlike Christmas, Easter was never assigned a fixed calendar date and remains based on a celestial event: the first Sunday after the first full moon following the spring equinox.

YULE

December 20-23
Winter Solstice,
Midwinter,
Saint Thomas' Day,
Festival of the Rebirth of the Sun,
Christmas (Dec. 25th),
Hanukkah (25 Kislev for 8 days),
Festival of Lights.

YULE

This longest night of the year was a pivotal point on the ancient calendar, for it heralded with its passing a return to the light half of the year. After this day, the hours of daylight become longer.

The concept of the sun as a conscious entity who experiences a rebirth each year is reflected in the mythology of several ancient cultures and religions: Helios, the Greek sun god; *Sol Invictus* or "Unconquered Sun" being the Roman equivalent; Mithras, a Persian deity; and Horus, the Egyptian sun-god. All were honored at festivals heralding the winter solstice.

Saturnalia, an ancient Roman festival in honor of the god Saturn, took place on December 17th and was essentially a day when the social roles of master and slave were reversed. It was celebrated with copious amounts of wine, feasting and gift-giving. The masters would serve the slaves, and the slaves were permitted to show disrespect toward their masters. The holiday gained so much popularity that it was eventually extended to a full seven days each year.

The Romans, however, also held a Yule festival called *Dies Natalis Solis Invicti* ("Birthday of the Unconquered Sun") on the winter solstice, which according to the Julian calendar occurred on December 25th. With the Yule feast occurring just after Saturnalia, the two celebrations eventually overlapped and were infused together as *Sol Invictus.* Centuries later, the early Roman Catholic Church under Pope Julius I designated the date of the winter solstice as the birthday of Christ in order to incorporate the Roman's favorite pagan festival. Thus, we have Christmas.

In Scandinavian tradition, the celebration of *Jul* or *Jōl* involves the *Joulupukki* or "yule-goat," who arrives in a sleigh pulled by a reindeer as he comes bearing gifts for the children of the household. In earlier times it was also common practice to sacrifice a boar or pig to the sun-god on this day, hence the modern tradition of eating a ham on Christmas. In past times, *Jul* actually incorporated several wintertime celebrations, during which time family and friends would meet to exchange gifts and drink together. This generally took place over a period of twelve days, hence the Twelve Days of Christmas.

Judisk Jul, or "Jewish Yule" referring to Hanukkah, is celebrated over an eight day period and is also called the "Festival of Lights". The dates of observance do not follow the Gregorian Calendar, and like so many other celestial-based holidays the dates are transitory. Hanukkah may begin anywhere from late-November to late-December. Similar to the Celtic calendar, the days of the Hebrew calendar begin and end with the setting of the sun, rather than at midnight.

In Germanic lore, the solstice is personified as a contrast between the Holly King (the Dark King, or god of the waning year) and his counterpart, the Oak King (also called the Child of Light, or god of the waxing year). The Holly King is sacrificed, and the Oak King ascends to reign for the light half of the year, until Litha, the summer solstice, when the two will trade hierarchies once again. In Celtic lore, the sun god Cernunnous (also known as the "Horned God" or "Forest King") is depicted as a man bearing the antlers of a deer.

Evergreen trees, found in abundance throughout northern lands, were considered magical, as they continued to thrive while others withered at this dead time of year. The evergreen and other hearty winter plants like mistletoe and holly were symbols of nature's survival and heralds the rebirth of the sun. The custom of decorating with evergreens and the like is carried through today with Christmas trees and wreaths.

IMBOLC
February 2
Beginning of Spring,
Celtic Candle Festival,
Bride's Day,
Feast of Saint Brigid,
Purification of the Virgin,
Candlemas.

Imbolc (pronounced "im-molk") is a festival that heralds the promise of Spring and honors the Celtic goddess Brigid (also Bridget or Bride, Bridhe, Brid, the latter pronounced "breed"). According to legend, it is Brigid who keeps the fires of the Earth stoked, firing them when it is time for Nature to be reborn.

In honor of Brigid, a perpetual, sacred flame is tended to by an order of nuns at a sanctuary in Kildare, Ireland. It is said that the flame has burned longer than even the existence of Christianity, having once been maintained by Druid priestesses.

Christians recast the pagan goddess Brigid as Saint Bridget of Kildare, and assigned her festival day as Saint Bridget's Day. And, being that Brigid was the goddess of poetry, smithwork and healing, so Saint Bridget came to be the patron saint of these arts as well.

This day is also celebrated in Christian tradition as the Feast of the Purification of the Virgin, or Candlemas, during which candles are lighted at midnight, commemorating the presentation of the infant Jesus at Temple and the purification of the Virgin Mary. According to Jewish law, the mother of a male child had to be purified by ritual 40 days after the birth.

In Wiccan tradition, Imbolc is the point at which the old aspect of the Goddess, the Crone, is transformed once again into the Maiden. Some fertility rites refer to the making ready of the seeds of life, firing them so they stir again in the cold earth, and to the purification of the Maiden so that she is prepared to conceive.

OSTARA
March 20-23
Spring Equinox,
Celtic Bird Festival,
The Annunciation,
Easter.

OSTARA

Ostara marks a turning point from the dark to the light half of the year. After this point the days will grow longer. It is the time to sow the seeds that will later bear fruit, a good time to set in motion any new plans.

Ostara is so named after the Germanic goddess of spring and fertility. According to Faerie lore, Ostara marks the time when the Wild Hunt, which has been out riding all winter, returns home to Faerie with its newly reborn leader, the young Forest King. As he matures, he will prepare to ride out once again to find his Queen.

Similar to Ostara is the goddess Eøstre, a fertility deity of Anglo-Saxon origin. Eøstre was represented by the egg and the rabbit, both of which are very obvious fertility symbols. The lunar festival honoring her was held on the first full moon that occurred on or after the vernal equinox. It was this goddess who is said to be the namesake for Easter, the Christian holiday devised by a Benedictine monk in the 8th century. The Church also re-envisioned the themes of resurrection and fertility as the day of the Annunciation, when the Virgin Mary was to have conceived Christ, and the Resurrection (Easter), when Jesus arose from the dead after the Crucifixion.

Today, the date of Easter is still determined by the Goddess' lunar cycle. It is marked on the calendar as the first Sunday following a full moon occurring on or after the vernal equinox.

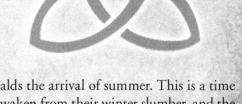

BELTANE
May 1
Beginning of Summer,
May Day,
Roodmas,
Celtic Flower Festival,
Walpurgis Night.

Beltane is a celebration of joy that heralds the arrival of summer. This is a time when nature blossoms, animals fully awaken from their winter slumber, and the land becomes fertile once again.

Lighting fires was customary on this day to honor a solar deity of Wales and Ireland, named Bel. Traditionally, the *Bel-fire* (or *bon-fire,* meaning "good fire") was composed of the nine sacred woods of the Celts: "Willows of the streams, Hazel of the rocks, Alder of the marches, Birch of the waterfalls, Ash of the shadows, Yew of the plain, Elm of the glens, Rowan of the mountains, and Oak of the sun."

Since the Celtic day started and ended at sundown, the Beltane celebration began at sunset on April 30th and continued until sunset on May 1. After extinguishing all hearth fires in the village, two Bel-fires were lit in a pasture or on a hilltop. Villagers would drive their livestock between the fires three times, purifying them to insure fertility, prosperity and protection.

The village would elect a virgin as their "May Queen." She represented the virgin Goddess on the eve of her transition from Maiden to Woman. Her Consort was called "Jack-in-the-Green," "Green Man," or the "May King." The King and Queen represented the God and Goddess, who would join together to create the Divine Child, who would be born at Yule.

During Beltane the standards of social etiquette were very much relaxed. It was customary for couples to make love in a freshly plowed field to bless the crops and the earth. The concept of monogamy was also pretty much dismissed during the evening festivities. The dance around the Maypole was believed to bring fertility and good fortune. The entwining of ribbons around the pole by the dancers symbolized the union between the God and the Goddess.

The festival is sometimes referred to as Roodmas, so named by the Church in an attempt to associate Beltane with the Cross (for which the medieval term was the "Rood") rather than the Maypole.

Beltane was also appropriated by the Church as the Feast Day of Saint Walpurga. Walpurga was a nun, an English missionary to the land of the Franks. She lived in a convent in Germany, where she died on February 25, 779. She was canonized on May 1.

It is said that on *Walpurgisnacht* the veil between life and death grows thin, and so bonfires are lit to keep the dead at bay. In Norse mythology, this night commemorates the time when Odin, after hanging from the sacred *Yggdrasill* tree for nine days, entered the realm of the dead where he gained the knowledge of the Runes.

Recently, modern pagans have incorporated the bonfire ritual with the burning of a human effigy, a "Burning Man" or "Wicker Man." A giant wooden skeletal structure of a man is erected in a field, stuffed with straw, and set aflame at sundown. The building of such an impressive structure can sometimes take days to complete and is a creative medium for the bonfire.

The Wicker Man, however, hearkens to a sinister rumor about supposed human sacrifices made by the Druids of Gaul during the reign of Julius Caesar. According to one historical account written by Caesar, the Gauls built such structures to imprison their criminals, then burned them alive as tribute to their gods. However, given that Caesar was at war against the Gauls at the time, his account is likely biased.

LITHA

June 20-23
Summer Solstice,
Midsummer,
Celtic Oak Festival,
Saint John the Baptist's Day.

Litha marks the longest day of the year, the pinnacle of summer. This solar festival celebrates the height of the sun's power and the abundance of nature. But this time is also a reminder that what goes up must also come down—for once the sun has reached its *apogee* (highest point in the sky) it can only decline from this day forward. After Litha, the days grow shorter. This decline is symbolized in Germanic lore by the crowning of the Oak King. At his crowning, the Oak King is sacrificed to his darker aspect, the Holly King.

Just as the winter solstice festival was appropriated by the Church to celebrate Christ's birth, so too was this festival taken to mark the birth of Saint John the Baptist. Typically, saints' days correspond to the dates of their deaths, but this day is unusual in that it commemorates his birth.

In pagan tradition, the King and Queen (God and Goddess) are joined in marriage, and Litha is the celebratory party that follows. Indeed, this season is a popular time for handfastings and weddings. A typical Midsummer festival includes drumming, dancing, singing and drinking. The full moon in June is known as the "Honey Moon," and mead is a traditional drink for Litha gatherings.

LUGHNASADH

August 1
Beginning of Autumn,
Celtic Grain Festival,
Lammas.

Lughnasadh (pronounced "loo-nus-uh") heralds the beginning of Autumn and the first of three harvest periods. Lughnasadh is the time when the grain crop is gathered and plants disperse their seeds in preparation for next year's growth cycle.

Lughnasadh is named after the Celtic sun god, Lugh (pronounced "loo"). Traditionally, the first loaf of bread made from crop gathered at this early harvest was eaten in thanks. This tradition was continued in the Christian Church as the Lammas or "loaf-mass" service, where the first loaf would be blessed at mass.

The pagan Goddess is depicted as the pregnant Earth Mother. The aging King begins to decline, becoming weaker as the days grow shorter, yet he is simultaneously existing as the Goddess' unborn child. Druidic tradition also tells of the Corn King being cut down to be sacrificed and transformed into the life-giving fruits of the harvest. Deities and symbols associated with agriculture and harvest were very important at this time of year.

Lughnasadh is a time to take stock of resources, a time to reap that which has been sown—be it for good or ill.

MABON
September 20-23
Fall Equinox,
Celtic Festival of the Vine,
Michaelmas,
Feast of Avalon,
Feast of Saint Matthew.

It is the midst of autumn, and the time of the second harvest is upon us, when fruits of the vine are ripe for the picking. In past times, the Druids would honor the Green Man or Forest King by an offering of libation to the sacred Trees.

MABON

The hours of day and night are perfectly balanced on Mabon, which is the turning point when the calendar enters the dark half of the year. Celtic mythology tells of the god Mabon the "divine son" who was abducted from his mother only days after his birth to be raised in the land of Annwn, the Underworld. This theme is later referred to in legend when King Arthur dies and is taken away to Avalon.

In keeping with the theme of the world having been "plunged into darkness" the Christians celebrate the Feast of Saint Michael and All Angels (Michaelmas) to honor the heavenly warriors Michael, Gabriel, and Raphael, who are charged with protecting the earthly realm against the dark of night.

SAMHAIN

October 31
Beginning of Winter,
Feast of the Dead,
Halloween,
Celtic New Year,
All Saints' Day,
Night of the Wild Hunt.

Samhain (pronounced "sow-en") marks the beginning of Winter. This is the time of the third and final harvest, which in earlier days meant that livestock was brought in from the summer pastures to be slaughtered. Meats were smoked or salted and other foodstuffs were stored in preparation for the cold days of winter.

Modern observances generally refer to this as "Celtic New Year," but the ancients most likely saw this time as the end or "death" of the year, while the "new" year was celebrated much as it is today, just after the winter solstice, when the light half of the year would follow, in keeping with the Celtic ideal that day follows night.

Samhain was a time for honoring the dead. This day was observed by the Gauls as the "Feast of the Dead." In the seventh century the Church established All Saints' Day for remembering those that were canonized, and All Soul's Day for every other deceased soul.

In Wiccan tradition, the aging Goddess is honored as she passes from Mother to Crone, and Faerie lore tells of the "Night of the Wild Hunt," when an array of mythical creatures, led by the Horned God, set out from Faerie to roam the countryside. Eventually, they make their descent into the Underworld, where the aging God enters his winter sleep, to arise again at Yule.

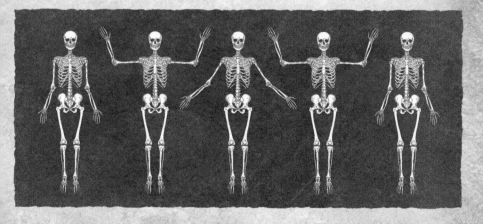

THE MYSTICAL POWERS OF THE YANTRA

The Yantra is a Hindu charm used for the fulfillment of dreams. It is a powerful talisman that is believed to bestow great blessings upon those who use it. Yantra designs are used to adorn temples and homes, assuring peace, harmony and spiritual bliss to all those within its realm of influence.

The Yantra

The Yantra is an ancient design that establishes a focus for meditation and inner reflection. The Yantra pattern consists of several concentric rings surrounded by an outer wall with four gates. Essentially, a Yantra is a two-dimensional representation of the cosmic landscape that surrounds all life. The central design represents the pinnacle of enlightenment. Each Yantra is personalized by its maker through the use of colors and symbols, creating a meditative focal point on one's personal altar.

Architectural Yantras are used to create sacred areas in temples. Such Yantras can take the form of painted wall hangings or intricate floor tile patterns that adorn areas of meditation. Yantra plaques made of brass are hung on walls to create positive energy environments in homes.

A Yantra is a geometrical pattern made of several concentric figures. This visual tool serves to free the consciousness during meditation by giving the mind something abstract to focus upon. It can either be a centering device or symbolic of divine energy patterns. The practice of using the Yantra began more than 2000 years ago in the Tantric tradition of India.

According to Tantric beliefs, the creation of the world began with the act of division—much like the first division of a single cell into that which will eventually become a higher life form—by which opposites (male and female) are divided yet are united in their goal.

The world is a continuous unfolding and expansion of energies, until a state is reached when the process must reverse and fold back upon itself to the very beginning. The same principles that apply to the expansion and contraction of universal energies are hence applied to the energies of the individual human being.

The Yantra is like a map of a person's spiritual journey, the ultimate goal of which is to ascend beyond one's basic existence and return to the center, the beginning. Each of the paths of the Yantra, from the outer plane to the center, correspond with a stage of enlightenment. Thus, the Yantra is a visual tool that aids a person in retracing his steps from the outer physical world to the inner spiritual realm, focusing and unifying mind and body through meditation.

A Meditation Tool

Oftentimes, meditation will combine the use of imagery, such as the Yantra, with a vocalized equivalent, called the *mantra*. While the Yantra symbolizes that which is physical, the mantra represents that which is invisible: the spirit or divine energy. Essentially, a Yantra is the physical expression of a mantra.

The act of drawing and painting a Yantra requires a high degree of accuracy and patience, and therefore aids concentration. While the geometrical forms of the Yantra activate the right hemisphere of the brain, which is typically associated with creativity and visual expression, the act of speaking a mantra exercises the left-brain. By combining Yantra and mantra in meditation, one's faculties are given balance, enabling one to achieve a calmer, higher state of awareness.

The Structure of a Yantra

Each part of the Yantra corresponds to a different aspect of the universe, the divine, or cosmos. According to Tantra the first expression of divine consciousness is conducted as the vibration of sound, the mantra. The following stage is physical manifestation, then come the various aspects of the physical.

The very first speck of physical matter is symbolized by the *bindu,* the central dot in the Yantra design. It signifies unity, the cosmos and origin. This point is the first step in meditation. To concentrate on this point brings the mind closer to abstract thought, which is used as a means to achieve higher awareness.

The circle is the natural extension of the point, and represents the creation of individual consciousness. The design then expands outward as rays, or aspects of the physical world, symbolized as other circles, triangles, squares, lotus petals and other variations on these basic shapes.

The first series of three rings represent the basic qualities of nature: balance, activity and inertia. Everything that exists in our universe manifests from different combinations and amounts of these three qualities.

The triangle is the next Yantra form and is symbolic of several things: the upward pointing triangle represents productive energy, that which is attributed to the male aspect, while the downward triangle symbolizes receptive energy, or that attributed to the feminine. The hexagon, created by the merging of the male and female triangles, represents more complex matter, division and growth from the original matter. It is this combination of the male and

female—equally represented, with no inferiority or superiority implied—that creates perfect balance and harmony.

A configuration called the Sri Yantra involves nine interlacing triangles, illustrated by the superimposition of five downward pointing triangles and four upright triangles. Aside from the divine masculine and feminine symbolism, it also includes reference to the five elements of nature: air, fire, water, earth and ether. The five senses: touch, taste, sight, smell, and hearing are also symbolized.

The lotus petals symbolize the expanding consciousness, much like a flower blossoming, as one nears complete enlightenment. Basic human aspirations are represented in the inner eight petals: abundance, love, recognition, health, spirituality, transformation, creativity and knowledge. The outer sixteen petals used in some designs represent aspects such as emotions, strength, wisdom, intellect and ego, traits such as austerity and self-sacrifice, and forms of energy such as desire and life-force.

The three rings surrounding the lotus blossoms represent the three planes of existence. Mankind exists in two: the physical world and the astral plane, the place of dreams. The realm of spirits and the divine exist in the causal world, a beautiful and magical realm that may be glimpsed by mankind only through proper meditation and ascension.

Everything is framed by a maze-like square that represents the infinity of creation, the four cardinal directions: north, south, east, and west, and the four gates by which one may enter the Yantra and aspire to ascension and unity.

Aside from the geometric Yantras there are numerical Yantras. These are based on a root number. A square is divided into nine equal parts with a number assigned to each block. All the numbers added in any direction vertically, horizontally, or diagonally add up to the same total sum.

MADAME ENDORA'S
FORTUNE CARDS

The fastest and easiest way to discover what your future holds

Madame Endora's Fortune Cards offer insightful advice concerning matters of love, money, health and general prosperity. The lush, symbolic artwork is based on Old World myth and lore, and blends Egyptian, Celtic and Fantasy themes in an elegant Art Nouveau style. Boxed set contains 48 cards, size 3x5.